NEGATIVE LAND

EDDY JOKOVICH

NP
NEW POLITICS

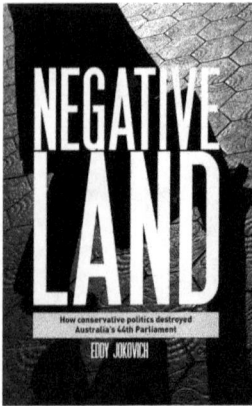

Negativeland: How conservative politics destroyed Australia's 44th parliament
ISBN: 978-0-9942154-0-6

🐦 @EddyJokovich

Published by New Politics
Cover design: Madeleine Preston

New Politics
PO Box 1265, Darlinghurst NSW 1300
www.newpolitics.com.au

Email: info@newpolitics.com.au

National Library of Australia Cataloguing-in-Publication entry
Creator: Jokovich, Eddy, author.

Title: Negative land : how conservative politics destroyed Australia's 44th parliament / Eddy Jokovich.

ISBN: 9780994215406 (paperback)

Subjects: Essays.
Conservatism--Australia.
Conservatism in the press--Australia.
Australia--Politics and government.

Contents

These essays were produced during Australia's 44th Parliament between 2013–2016 and offer insights into the performance of the Liberal–National Coalition, and the two Prime Ministers that presided during this time, Tony Abbott and Malcolm Turnbull.

The book commences in the week before the 2013 election— Labor Prime Minister Kevin Rudd is struggling to overcome three years of leadership turmoil in his party and the Liberal Party leader, Tony Abbott, is poised to win the election.

We travel through the bizarre nature of Tony Abbott's prime ministership, and how he couldn't make the transition from combative Leader of the Opposition to a Prime Minister with gravitas, where he could rise above petty ideological squabbles.

His replacement, Malcolm Turnbull, offered hope to the electorate, but ended up languishing in a position as poor as his predecessor's.

We explore the 2016 election campaign, ending with the aftermath, and ponder how conservative politicians and their supporters in the media have taken Australian politics to a point where the electorate is wondering whether our political leaders have the skills or the desire to lead Australia through difficult times.

July 2017

Election 2013: The final countdown

1 September 2013

The *Final Countdown* was a grand hit in 1986 by the Swedish band Europe and, finally, we have our own version of the final countdown: it's the final week of the 2013 election campaign, and while opinion polls (and betting markets) strongly favour a Liberal–National Coalition victory, many things can happen in these final seven days. The reason why I've started off with a music theme is that last night's screening of the ABC late-night music program *Rage*, was 'co-compered' by Labor Deputy Prime Minister, Anthony Albanese, the Coalition's Julie Bishop, and the Australian Greens' Adam Bandt. You really can judge character through musical choices, and my vote goes with Anthony Albanese, with a preference for Adam Bandt (sorry Julie, your song choices weren't great and you weren't going to get my vote anyway).

Anyhow, I digress. The Labor Party kick-started the final week of the campaign with a return to 'the Real Kevin', where the Prime Minister, Kevin Rudd, provided his best campaign moment, and left many wondering where he'd been over the past four weeks, or even the past three months.

Campaigns are all about momentum, and after four very uneven weeks, has Rudd finally righted the ship? Or is it a case of 'too-little, too-late'? This is likely the case, although there are many examples in recent Australian political history where the most favoured party failed to get over the line. The most memorable, of course, is Paul Keating's 'true believers' victory in 1993 where, at the start of the final week of campaigning, some polls were showing a two-party preferred vote of 45 per cent for Labor. Seven days later, Keating won the election.

Federally, it's not such a common event, but there are many examples at the state level: Western Australia (1989), where somehow, the Labor Party managed to hold onto government, despite many pundits predicting a loss as well as a 10 per cent swing against it; Victoria (1999), where Labor's Steve Bracks snuck into office, despite many predicting Liberal Premier Jeff Kennett maintaining office (Newspoll did detect a late swing in its last published poll on election day); Western Australia again (2001), where Labor's Geoff Gallop repeated the effort of Bracks, and snuck into office against Liberal Premier Richard Court; Queensland (2009), where Labor Premier Anna Bligh was expected to lose, but won the election by nine seats.

There's not much to suggest that anything will change during the week, especially with the unusual media intervention by News Limited during the campaign, culminating in the *Sunday Telegraph*'s front page lead on 1 September, 'Australia Needs Tony'.[1] This is one of their more bizarre interventions, rivaling any propaganda that might have adorned Communist-styled newspapers during the Cold War. In fact, change the language, name and face, and you'd be close to a propaganda poster released by former North Korean leader, Kim Jong-Il. It really was a pity that former Minister for Communications, Steven Conroy, didn't proceed with his reforms to clean up the media in Australia. These front-page interventions by News Limited,

---

1   ABC News, 'Sunday Telegraph front page', 1 September 2013. http://www.abc.net.au/news/2013-09-01/sunday-telegraph-front-page-september-1-2013/4927412

through their Liberal Party megaphones, *The Courier Mail*, *Daily Telegraph* and *The Australian* have been over the top and, if you removed their respective mastheads, could easily double up as *Honi Soit* covers controlled by the Sydney University Young Liberals.

In fact, most of the Coalition's campaign has resembled a strategy devised by Young Liberals completing their final year political science assignments. Devoid of any vision, but rambling around the same three key messages: things will always be better under a Coalition government, turning back the boats, and getting the budget back into surplus (although, this has been revised to include 'buying the boats' and 'controlling the budget'). Perhaps the Liberal campaign headquarters realised that Tony Abbott had created so many landmines and backrods for a future Coalition government that their messages had to be pared back.

In his interview with Barry Cassidy on the ABC *Insiders* this morning, Tony Abbott mentioned that there would be 'no surprises and no excuses in government'. If nothing else, the Labor Party must keep these utterances in its dossier for their time in Opposition (if it comes to that), over the next three years. Abbott has been relentlessly negative since he became Leader of the Opposition in 2009, has offered no real indications for what the Liberals will do in government (other than saying that 'things will be better than Labor') and no policy costings. This really is dangerous and, as the ALP has been warning, could result in a 'Campbell Newman approach' (where the newly-installed Premier of Queensland implemented a harsh reactionary agenda) applied throughout Australia.

Bringing out the scare campaign in the final week might not do enough for Labor, but let's keep a look out for any last minute slip-ups.

*

As expected, the Liberal–National Party easily won the 2013 election on 2 September, picking up 18 seats and a 53.49 per cent of the two-party prefered vote. A landslide. The electorate decided that the ongoing leadership instability in the Labor Party had to be punished, resulting in Labor's lowest primary vote since the 1931 election—when James Scullin's government lost office during the peak of the depression—and its lowest two-party preferred vote since 1996, when Paul Keating's government was voted out.

Strangely for a government that had just suffered a massive defeat, Kevin Rudd's concession speech felt more like a victory, somehow more euphoric compared to his winning election result in 2007—perhaps all he wanted was to reclaim the Prime Ministership after it was abruptly taken away from him in June 2010 in a late night leadership coup that installed Julia Gillard as leader, and he'd achieved that. Whatever happened at the election might have been irrelevant to him.

Tony Abbott became the new Prime Minister, but he's created so made rods for his back that this first term will be difficult to manage politically. The new government seemed to be in lock-down mode for several months after the election, with not too much happening within the electoral cycle. Exhaustion from such a vicious period of negative politics? Laziness? Time will tell.

Just after the election, Kevin Rudd resigned from Parliament, and Bill Shorten became leader of the Labor Party—ironic, since he was the prime mover in the subterranean campaign to remove Rudd from the leadership in 2010, and again, to remove Julia Gillard in 2013.

Historically, a newly appointed Leader of the Opposition immediately after a crushing election loss has a thankless task. It's usually at least two parliamentary terms of arduous work—if they manage to survive that long—and low expectations mean that they're always one or two errors away from the scrapheap. Bill Shorten has won virtually every political contest he's been up against but, this time around, he's up against an unconvinced electorate, and a febrile conservative media that has decided that he ain't their man. It will be interesting to see how he can survive.

A government not in control of itself

9 January 2014

How does one describe the performance of the Abbott government since its election in September last year? While it has been verging on the chaotic and, to use the terminology the Liberal–National Party was using against the Labor Party during the last Parliament, 'shambolic', it's too early to see how this will affect the rest of its term.

There are many areas where it has either dismantled a Labor-initiated program (Better Schools); broken its promises (by suggesting a $7 co-payment for visits to a doctor; presiding over a 6 per cent increase in health premiums), or instigated bizarre practices, such as the media clampdown on Operation Border Security, or seeking a 'media truce'[1] after a few journalists reported the purchase of new VIP jets worth $250 million, while the government cut essential services for vulnerable people.

The electorate can be forgiving when a new government is installed, and mishaps can always be ignored early in the term.

1 *North Coast Voices*, 'Now Abbott wants to spend an est. $250 million on his own VIP air transport while ripping funding from vulnerable Australians', 6 January 2014. http://northcoastvoices.blogspot.com.au/2014/01/now-abbott-wants-to-spend-est-250.html

Former Liberal Prime Minister John Howard's first term in 1996–98 was littered with mistakes and ministerial resignations, but it clicked midway through the term (at this point, the Coalition was polling nationally at around 45 per cent, two-part preferred), he promoted the goods and services tax agenda, developed the idea of being the 'conviction' politician and managed to win the 1998 election. It's hard to see where Abbott's agenda is going to come from—whether a government is conservative or progressive, implementing an agenda is a creative process and involves thought processes at a level higher than three-word mantras. Dismantling a predecessor's agenda and behaving like it's 1978 at the University of Sydney Student Representative Council simply won't work for the electorate.

There is barely a day that goes by where there isn't a bad news story for the Liberal–National Party—this week has seen the release of Senator Cory Bernardi's *The Conservative Revolution*, a tome containing a far-right agenda that has been openly mocked on Amazon[2] and created divisions with the Coalition. I've read it and for what it's worth, it's a poorly written publication that would be more in tune with the revolutionary times of Iran in the late 1970s. It just doesn't have a place in contemporary Australia (or any other contemporary place in the world). Its purpose is probably for Tony Abbott to 'triangulate', by having one of his own push forward an extreme agenda and then take the middle ground (or at least have more 'common sense' than Bernardi is displaying).

And then there's the ongoing stoush with Indonesia over boats and asylum seekers. It's difficult to know exactly what is happening here, because the Australian Government is so intent on providing as little information as possible, under the guise of 'operational matters'. This week saw the allegations that the Australian Navy maltreated Somali and Sudanese

---

2   Amazon, customer reviews, 1 November 2013. http://www.amazon.com/the-conservative-revolution-Cory-Bernardi/product-reviews/1922168963/ref=dp_top_cm_cr_acr_txt?showViewpoints=1

asylum seekers[3] and towed their boats for five days back into Indonesian waters. Whether or not asylum seekers are legal or not, there are basic human rights that should be respected, and government maltreating people in such a way is unacceptable.

The 'flavour' of a government takes a while to settle. But the Abbott government has used up more than 10 per cent of this parliamentary term and has not gone past the negative agenda that it promoted during the last Parliament and the 2013 election campaign. Once perceptions set in, it's difficult to change those perceptions, as Julia Gillard discovered during her time as Prime Minister. We'll get a better understanding of what the long-term future for the Abbott government will be after the Budget is released in May but, so far, it's not looking very promising.

*

3   ABC News, 'Tony Abbott happy to be 'closed book' on border operations as Labor demands details on asylum boat turn-backs', 4 February 2014. http://www.abc.net. au/news/2014-01-09/indonesian-military-chief-discussed-boat-turnbacks-with-adf-boss/5191486

Tony Abbott: Bad Prime Minister

3 February 2014

My wife's young nephew and niece visited during the Christmas school holidays and, as most children do when they're from a different part of Australia, introduced some of their local vernacular. Coming from the conservative heartland of the Riverina, they demonstrated what the 'outsider' kids are doing: whenever mentioning Tony Abbott, they mutter behind one hand, in a softer secret whisper: 'bad Prime Minister'. Sometimes, they'll extend their repertoire: 'Julia Gillard: OK Prime Minister'. Sometimes: 'Kevin Rudd: OK Prime Minister'. And on the very odd occasion: 'Paul Keating: Good Prime Minister.' Now, there's a Prime Minister worth respecting.

Of course, they are being inculcated by their families and their small peer group, but it's amusing listening to nine- and 10-years-olds act out their subversive behaviour amongst the conservatives. I'm not sure about Julie Gillard: I'd say she was 'so-so', but I don't believe she was anywhere near as bad as her critics made out, or as bad as her poll numbers suggest. I believe history will be kind to Gillard and behind the facade of the brutal politics during 2010–2013 is a list of policy programs of substance (which, of course, are just about to be destroyed by the Liberal–National government), delivered in a hostile hung Parliament, which very few Prime Ministers could have survived.

But, poll numbers are what politicians are judged on, so her ratings get the thumbs down. Kevin Rudd was a disaster as Prime Minister. A ten-year period of government awaited the Labor Party but Rudd, although he had great potential, couldn't manage the party. And, therefore, the party couldn't manage him. And the person who did the most damage, Bill Shorten, is now leading their party.

Tony Abbott? Is he 'bad'? If so, how bad is he really as a Prime Minister?

My feeling is that this is going to be one hell of a bad Prime Minister. Of course, we don't know what a Prime Minister will be like until they reach the position but looking at Abbott in the first four months of this term, his past and his background, suggests that he's on track to being one of the worst and most divisive Prime Minister this country has seen. The most divisive? We'll get to this later.

Abbott comes from a very privileged background, attending St Aloysius' College in primary school and the prestigious St Ignatius' College in secondary school. His father was an orthodontist, and established one of the largest practices in Australia. He has, pretty much, had everything laid out for him, even when the going gets tough. During his time at the University of Sydney, he was charged with the indecent assault of a female student. He was also caught by police vandalising a traffic sign. On both occasions, he was lawyered up and both charges were dismissed. And this has been symptomatic of most of his adult life: when difficult times arrive, he eschews personal responsibility and seeks protection, either through the law (for example, the defamation case against author Bob Ellis in 1998 for allegations made in the book *Goodbye Jerusalem*, or through powerful benefactors, such as media mogul Rupert Murdoch.

There is nothing in Tony Abbott's public persona or history to suggest we have someone who brings gravitas to the office of Prime Minister, and few qualities of decency. His comments as Minister for Health about asbestos activist and campaigner Bernie Banton during the 2007 election campaign[1] are probably the best indication of his persona and character: First, slurring a dying man suffering from mesothelioma (saying "just because a person is sick doesn't mean that he [Banton] is necessarily pure of heart") and refusing to meet with him to discuss a compensation plan for sufferers of asbestosis, but then blaming his own staff for a 'mix-up', saying it was their fault the meeting with Banton didn't proceed. No responsibility.

Now comes that bad part. Democracy, of course, is about representation, and when a specific party comes to office, they represent their supporter base; in the case of the Liberal Party, small and large business. Tony Abbott used to be a journalist. He worked for News Limited. The chairman and CEO of News Limited, Rupert Murdoch supported the Liberal–National Party election campaign with some of the most one-sided and over-the-top journalism ever, through his mouthpieces, the *Daily Telegraph*, *Herald Sun*, *Courier Mail* and *The Australian*.

Tony Abbott represents business people in Parliament, and his business philosophies are in tune with rabid right-wing economic orthodoxies of the worst kind. If it were not for the rule of law and the restraints of Parliament, liberal economic philosopher Friedrich Hayek's dogma would be considered to be too weak, and we'd be all on the road to serfdom again. Just like a production line in a sausage factory, labour would be offered and paid as required: no holiday pay, no sick leave. If you're not required for the following day, you are told so. You go back to work when the employer contacts you. If you don't like what's being offered, you go somewhere else.

Forget all the analysis about Abbott being a semi-Democratic Labor-ite, and wanting people to have at least some sort of safety

1   Ben Doherty, *The Age*, 'Abbott adamant over Banton 'stunt'', 31 October 2007. http://www.theage.com.au/news/federalelection2007news/abbott-adamant-over-banton-stunt/2007/10/31/1193618926085.html

net for the social good. If Abbott can go to a place where the labour market is totally de-regulated and de-unionised, he will go there. And, as if he is channeling the spirit of the National Civic Council's B.A. Santamaria, he is now attacking the ABC for 'not supporting the home team' and lacking patriotism in its news reporting.

On workplace relations, the rhetoric coming from both Abbott and his Minister for Employment, Senator Eric Abetz, has been gratuitous, vile and incorrect.[2] Australia is not on the verge of a 'wages blowout'. Since The Accords from 1983 until 1991[3] (Marks 1–7), wages have been kept in check. Abbott's criticism of the employment conditions at SPC Ardmona[4] being 'overly generous' and needing to be cut back shows that his government is preparing for an assault on working environments across Australia. And this follows on from claiming that Holden workers losing their jobs in 2017 could be a 'liberating experience'. No sympathy.

And, in-between the domestic political mishaps, there have been the international disasters with Indonesia, and the spat over the East China Sea with Chinese foreign minister Wang Li. These incidents have arisen through arrogance and incompetence. Diplomatic relationships can be smoothed over through time: countries are pragmatic and self-interested when it comes to trade but these are incidents that were unnecessary and poorly managed. Again, the mainstream media came to the rescue, ensuring that both incidents were glossed over for domestic audiences.

---

2   Naomi Woodley, ABC News, 'Eric Abetz warns of wages 'explosion' unless employers stop 'caving in' to unions', 29 January 2014. http://www.abc.net.au/news/2014-01-29/eric-abetz-warns-of-wages-breakout/5224382

3   Anthony Forsyth & Carolyn Holbrook, *The Conversation*, 'Australian politics explainer: the Prices and Incomes Accord', 24 April 2017. http://theconversation.com/australian-politics-explainer-the-prices-and-incomes-accord-75622

4   James Massola, Jonathan Swan, Judith Ireland, Georgia Wilkins, *Sydney Morning Herald*, 'Cabinet rejects SPC Ardmona's bid for $25 million assistance', 30 January 2014. http://www.smh.com.au/federal-politics/political-news/cabinet-rejects-spc-ardmonas-bid-for-25-million-assistance-20140130-31p4e.html

However, on another new level of arrogance was the speech Abbott made at the Word Economic Forum in Davos,[5] where amongst the business intellectuals of the world, he announced platitudes such as: "you can't spend what you haven't got"; "a certain level of government spending is necessary and good"; "profit is not a dirty word—because success in business is something to be proud of"; and "no country has ever taxed or subsidised its way to prosperity"…

Just who was that speech aimed at? For a domestic audience? Surely, there aren't enough naive people in Australia to be receptive to that type of economic simplicity. It was dreadful. It was woeful. The small business shopkeeper mentality came to the fore. And it would be no way to manage a country's economy.

Yet, the mainstream media reported this as some kind of economic revelation, bravery, and setting the course for a brilliant economic future. A more critical and accurate assessment of Abbott's performance comes from Mike Seccombe at *The Global Mail.*[6]

Man of substance? Man of convenience, more likely. And, he's not the family man that he would have you believe. A politician's private life should remain private and, whenever I've come across any juicy gossip about any politician, I've ignored it. And I normally would but it's about time Tony Abbott's marital life was placed under the same scrutiny that Julia Gillard was placed under: The disgusting and relentless diatribes from the *Pickering Post,*[7] her reputation besmirched, questions about her partner Tim Matheison's sexuality[8] and whether their

5   Dennis Shanahan, *The Australian*, 'Tony Abbott tells Davos: let business lead way', 23 January 2014. http://www.theaustralian.com.au/national-affairs/tony-abbott-tells-davos-let-business-lead-way/news-story/cd7cb17e4f5c202f02d39b5039fcb24f

6   Mike Seccombe, *The Global Mail*, 'Abbott's Davos Moment', 31 January 2014. Accessed at http://theworker1891.blogspot.com.au/2014/01/abbotts-davos-moment.html

7   Larry Pickering, *The Pickering Post*, 'Why Single Women Prefer Married Men', 23 September 2012. http://pickeringpost.com/story/why-single-women-prefer-married-men/597

8   Katharine Murphy, *The Guardian*, 'Julia Gillard asked by radio station if her partner Tim

relationship was a sham. It was relentless from the time she assumed the Prime Ministership in 2010. And we are yet to see any proposals for a Tony Abbott television sitcom akin to the ABC's *At Home With Julia*,[9] which lampooned the life of Julia Gillard and Tim Matheison at The Lodge in Canberra.

The mainstream media protects Abbott's personal life. Where are the questions about his alleged 18-month relationship with his Chief-of-Staff, Peta Credlin? It's an open secret amongst people 'in the know' in Canberra. Why was Julia Gillard's personal life aggressively targeted and constantly trashed, whereas Tony Abbott remains immune?

Why has the rather odd situation of Abbott staying at the Australian Federal Police flats[10] in Canberra not been scrutinised further? The Lodge is currently being renovated, but a leased family home which was meant to house Abbott and his family, costing over $156,000 until 31 August, remains empty. And why isn't any radio host asking Tony Abbott directly about his rumoured separation from Margie Abbott, in the same way that Julia Gillard was blatantly asked about her relationship?

The protection of Tony Abbott has existed all of his life, and continues in high office. He has protection from powerful players in the media. And this, coupled with classic conservative divisiveness and opportunism means that the next three years before the next election, due in 2016, will deteriorate even further.

Progressive politics offers creative solutions to society's problems. Conservative politics offers no creative solutions, and depends on reactionary divisiveness to maintain a grip on power. As John Howard showed in his time in office during

Mathieson is gay', 13 June 2013. http://www.theguardian.com/world/2013/jun/13/julia-gillard-howard-sattler-interview

9   Wikipedia, 'At Home With Julia'. http://en.wikipedia.org/wiki/At_Home_With_Julia

10   Samantha Maiden, *The Sunday Telegraph*, 'Tony Abbott abandons possum-infested Lodge in Canberra to live with AFP recruits until renovations are complete', 14 September 2013. http://www.dailytelegraph.com.au/news/nsw/tony-abbott-abandons-possuminfested-lodge-in-canberra-to-live-with-afp-recruits-until-renovations-are-complete/story-fni0cx12-1226719229780

1996–2007, a vacuum bereft of ideas can always be quickly filled with nationalistic jingoism, casual racism, asylum seekers, class warfare and attacks on unions (usually blue collar workers or the lowly paid). We know what Abbott is against, but we don't yet know what he is for. He will dismantle programs, but he won't build. He'll target vulnerable people, the ones that can't fight back. His entire agenda is based on a pay-back mentality that hasn't matured politically since his student days at the University of Sydney.

My wife's nephew and niece cautioned against a conservative government, claiming that 'they will make us go to school on Saturday', quickly followed by a surreptitious swipe: 'Tony Abbott: Bad Prime Minister'. Is Tony Abbott a 'bad Prime Minister'? In my opinion, the answer is yes, I think he is. But the storm clouds are still brewing. This is the time before the rain and the worst is yet to come.

*

The 'stop drownings at sea mantra' cloaks a racist agenda

26 February 2014

Boats, boats, boats. That's pretty much what the Liberal–National government put on offer during the 2013 election campaign. Sure, it's a message that was carefully melded into the carbon tax and Labor leadership chaos but, essentially, the biggest point of Tony Abbott's political differentiation was 'stop the boats'. And, if you didn't hear it loudly enough, it was littered throughout campaign paraphernalia and the Coalition's centrepiece booklet, 'Our Plan: Real Solutions for all Australians'.

The results of this mantra? Look no further than the incidents on Manus Island in Papua New Guinea, where some asylum seekers have died from infections after minor injuries and illnesses.[1] Playing politics with asylum seekers arriving by boat has reaped great dividends for the Coalition but where are the roots of the current crisis on Manus? Are its antecedents contained within the White Australia policy to exclude Kanaks from the domestic labour market? Former Liberal Prime

---

1   ABC News, 'Manus Island death: New information suggests detainee's fatal injury suffered inside detention centre', 23 February 2014. http://www.abc.net.au/news/2014-02-22/immigration-minister-scott-morrison-casts-doubt-on-manus-death/5277684

Minister Robert Menzies and his 'yellow peril' mania and anti-Communist rhetoric in the 1950s? Former ALP Minister for Immigration, Gerry Hand, and the introduction of 'mandatory detention' in 1992? Or the debacle in 2001, where John Howard refused entry to 433 asylum seekers stranded aboard the Norwegian freighter *MV Tampa*?

While these events make a contribution to the eternal Australian phobia with the outside world and the prospect of invasion from the north, the crisis on Manus Island has its roots back in 1998, when a freshly re-elected Liberal–National government decided that its future electoral prospects lay in the issue of asylum seekers, unauthorised boat arrivals and the so-called 'illegal' immigration. This is the time when then Minister for Immigration, Philip Ruddock, claimed 'whole villages... packing up' their suitcases in the Middle East were coming to Australia. Politics, since this time, has been bereft of ideas on asylum seekers, and is as further away as ever in being able to implement reasonable, humanitarian or creative solutions.

The greatest issue is not the boats. It's not the asylum seekers and it's not even the people smugglers. It's the political class that has provided weak and lazy leadership and, after 16 years of endless rhetoric about asylum seekers, the issue is more vexed than at the height of the Tampa stand-off in August 2001.

There are 226 federal parliamentarians, 76 in the Senate and 150 in the House of Representatives. Most, if not all, are university educated. Yet, the issue of asylum seekers has become almost more intractable than the Israel–Palestine question, and set in place another decade of partisan and inane policy responses. If placing asylum seekers in an expensive little orange boat and towing them by navy vessel to Indonesia[2] is the best that we can do, well, we're simply not trying hard enough.

Ruddock, after those relatively innocuous comments in

---

2   ABC News via YouTube, 'Video appears to show lifeboat being towed by an Australian vessel under Operation Sovereign Borders', 6 February 2014. http://youtu.be/TaTp2RCOe8I

1998, ramped up the rhetoric in 2000 by producing a series of videos, warning would-be asylum seekers that they would be 'eaten, bitten or mauled' by wild animals, if they took the voyage across seas to land in Australia.[3] He sold his soul in exchange for cheap applause at the 2001 Liberal Party election campaign launch. He is now lingers in federal Parliament as the 'Father of the House' and still wears an Amnesty International badge, as if he's reminding himself, and anyone else that might be interested, that there's some skerrick of light in that deep darkened soul. Good luck with that exploration.

Ruddock was also the first Minister for Immigration to start classifying asylum seeking as an illegal act, even though the *Migration Act* didn't support this proposition, nor was it supported by the United Nations' Refugee Convention, which Australia is a signatory to. This needs to be explained yet again: asylum seekers arriving by boat (or any other method) are not 'illegal' (although current Minister for Immigration, Scott Morrison did direct the Department of Immigration to use the terms '*illegal* maritime arrivals', rather than '*irregular* maritime arrivals' from October 2013 onwards).

In reality, prospective asylum seekers are classified as unlawful non-citizen arrivals and remain so until their credentials are determined. If they are found to be genuine asylum seekers, they remain in Australia. If not, it is at this point that they are defined as illegal and deported at the first opportunity or, if this is not possible, incarcerated in a migration detention facility.

This legal status has been consistently ignored by Coalition members of Parliament and there seems to be a warped sense of pride in the levels that asylum seekers can be demonised. Current Minister for Immigration Scott Morrison is in his element—he appears as a smiling cadaver, no doubt hoping for the same applause accorded to Ruddock, but we're yet to see

---

3   Nick Squires, *The Telegraph*, 'Australia uses its wildlife to scare away refugees', 18 June 2000, http://www.telegraph.co.uk/news/worldnews/australiaandthepacific/australia/1343756/Australia-uses-its-wildlife-to-scare-away-refugees.html

what his reward from this Faustian pact will be. A promotion perhaps at the time of the next Cabinet reshuffle or a keen diplomatic posting post-retirement?

The most disturbing development of this recent chapter in the handling of asylum seekers in Australia can be found in the new catchcry: stopping drownings at sea. It camouflages a fundamentally racist policy by making our vainglorious leaders seem concerned about the humanitarian impact of people making the journey across high seas, ostensibly putting our grand intentions of saving people from drowning first,[4] while relegating the racist intention of excluding these people and ensuring they never reach our shores to a secondary position.

The notion of 'stopping drownings at sea' developed currency during former Prime Minister, Julia Gillard's botched attempt at the 'Malaysia solution' in 2011, where Malaysia would accept 800 asylum seekers from Australia, in exchange of 4,000 'processed' refugees residing in Malaysia. It was at this time that Tony Abbott and Joe Hockey started claiming the most important issue was to 'stop drownings at sea'. Hockey was most vocal at this time about the issue,[5] stating 'one evil should not be compounded by another evil by a government', even crying on the floor of Parliament. He hasn't had much to say about the issue recently but, perhaps he's been too busy worrying about ending the age of entitlement.

'Stopping drownings at sea' also found its way into the *Report of the Expert Panel on Asylum Seekers*, released in August 2012, but after 18 months, the results of policy can be seen to be immoral and practically flawed. Its policy contradictions and duplicity make it a cross between Hannah Arrendt's *The Banality of Evil*

---

4   Craig Emerson, *The Australian*, 'I can live with being a heartless bastard if it stops the drownings', 27 July 2013. http://www.theaustralian.com.au/opinion/i-can-live-with-being-a-heartless-bastard-if-it-stops-the-drownings/news-story/392426ca9efb16d6498179403538838c

5   News.com.au, 'Malaysia child transfer evil, says Joe Hockey as Government begins people swap deal', 5 August 2011. http://www.news.com.au/breaking-news/malaysia-child-transfer-evil-says-joe-hockey-as-government-begins-people-swap-deal/story-e6frfku0-1226108823400

and Franz Kafka's *The Trial*. In the act of supposedly 'stopping drownings at sea', we will capture asylum seekers at sea, either tow them back to Indonesia like live cattle or incarcerate them, and implement such a wicked and hateful regime against them. And all of this from the hand of bureaucrats in central Canberra, with the imprimatur of a Prime Minister desperate to be able to continue announcing 'I stopped the boats'.

What the proponents of the Manus Island and Nauru options never outline is that while we're supposedly rescuing asylum seekers and deterring them from making the hazardous journey by sea, we're punishing those that make the journey by placing them in unsafe environments—apparently, our humanitarian concern is so great that we're prepared to implement an inhumane solution to arrive at a humane conclusion. A bit like destroying the Bến Tre village during the Vietnam war to save the village. Or, to destroy the soul to save the soul.

It's akin to selecting a group of law abiding Australian citizens and sending them to the Abu Ghraib prison in Iraq to deter the rest of the population from committing crime. Or someone running from a rampaging murderer on the street, knocking on your door, you decide to lock that person up in your bathroom, and then invite neighbours to throw rocks and sticks at them. And eventually kill them.

There are major problems with Tony Abbott's approach to asylum seekers on boats. The entire policy of off-shore processing and Operation Sovereign Borders has been shrouded in secrecy, and whatever information does become available, is littered with errors and misinformation. Abbott even likened his government's treatment of asylum seekers to being 'at war' with an enemy,[6] ironic, considering asylum seekers arriving by boat are fleeing real wars in Sri Lanka, Afghanistan, Iraq and Sudan.

6   Jonathan Swan, *Sydney Morning Herald*, 'Tony Abbott compares secrecy over asylum seekers to war time', 10 January 2014. http://www.smh.com.au/federal-politics/political-news/tony-abbott-compares-secrecy-over-asylum-seekers-to-war-time-20140110-30lyt.html

So, where does leave us? The recent incidents at Manus Island and Nauru indicate the policies are not sustainable. It's as though Abbott and Morrison are extending Philip Zimbardo's Stanford prison experiment,[7] permitting extended sessions of torture to see how far institutionalised abuse can be carried out.

I'm not seeking to change opinions within the electorate, because the ideas about asylum seekers are so entrenched and immovable within the community that it's almost not worth the bother. It's obvious that while there are many in the Australian community that are deeply concerned about the treatment of asylum seekers and the policy course the Coalition government has taken, there are many others that would prefer even harsher treatment, as shown in the Essential Media Communications report, 'Too soft or too tough on asylum seekers'.[8]

But when we have sight of the Chinese Government taking Australia to task for human rights abuse of asylum seekers and the Minister for Foreign Affairs, Julie Bishop, attempting to deal with Hun Sen, the Prime Minister of Cambodia, which is one of the poorest countries in the world, to take receive Australia's asylum seekers, we know that there is a great deal wrong and something needs to be done.

*

7   Social Psychology Network, Stanford prison experiment. http://www.prisonexp.org
8   Essential Media Communications, *Essential Report*, 'Too soft or too tough on asylum seekers', 21 January 2014. http://essentialvision.com.au/too-soft-or-too-tough-on-asylum-seekers-2

A very Australian conservative coup

8 June 2014

Much has been mentioned about the military coup in Thailand last month, but there has been a more significant attempted coup, albeit a silent one, closer to home. Yes, an Australian coup. And it's unlikely to succeed.

Since its election in September 2013, the Liberal–National Party has implemented the silent coup, displaying all the hallmarks of a military dictatorship. 'Oh, come on', you might say, 'that only happens in the countries of Asia and South America'.

Of course, military dictatorships have many features. They implement a radical agenda, usually conservative. They control the media, tell lies, have contempt for the general population, they are secretive, they place children and babies in prisons, they manipulate and use the rule of law to place their opponents in jail, they apply favourable rules to themselves and draconian rules for all others; and, lastly, seek grand benefit for family members.

Military dictatorships also have the hallmark of the political class operating within a vacuum, where they can neither hear nor understand the concerns of the community, and proceed to implement their agenda, 'for the good of the country'.

'Oh, come on', you say again. 'That sounds like North Korea. That couldn't possibly happen in Australia.'

But it is, and there are many similarities between undesirable military *juntas* and the Liberal–National Party. Firstly, in the tradition of State Peace and Development Council of Burma, People's Soviet Republic and Democratic Republic of Congo, the use of 'Liberal National' is classic doublespeak—the Liberal–National Party has all the hallmarks of a vicious right-wing conservative party, and very few of what would usually considered to be liberal.

First and foremost, the Liberal–National Party, has implemented a radical agenda, under the guise of a 'National Budget State of Emergency'.

It has adopted a style of political trickery and control tactics similar to those used by the military *junta* of Burma, answers to no-one, has control of the media (and vice versa, most notably News Limited, but also Fairfax Media and, increasingly, the ABC, are in thrall of the government), uses bribes and pay-offs for political favours, has contempt for the general populace, places young children and babies in immigration detention centres forever,[1] and seeks grand benefit for family members[2]— there are no limits for personal aggrandisement.

It uses the military to implement its agenda (using Lieutenant General Angus Campbell to 'assist' with Operations Sovereign Borders[3]), especially for secretive 'on-water' matters, and has achieved its own constitutional safeguards by installing a former

1   Melissa Sweet, *Crikey*, 'Inside the immigration detention facilities in Darwin: breeding grounds for mental illness', 17 December 2013. http://blogs.crikey.com.au/croakey/2013/12/17/inside-the-immigration-detention-facilities-in-darwin-breeding-grounds-for-mental-illness

2   James Law, News.com.au, 'Whitehouse Institute of Design under fire again over Frances Abbott scholarship with vandalism and protests', 28 May 2014. http://www.news.com.au/national/whitehouse-institute-of-design-under-fire-again-over-frances-abbott-scholarship-with-vandalism-and-protests/story-fncynjr2-1226934527875

3   Stefanie Balogh, *The Australian*, 'Tony Abbott's border general Angus Campbell promoted', 19 September 2013. http://www.theaustralian.com.au/national-affairs/policy/tony-abbotts-border-general-angus-campbell-gets-new-rank/story-e6frg8yo-1226722795077

military leader as the head of state,[4] Peter Cosgrove. This Liberal–National Party applies favourable rules for itself, and draconian rules for all others.

It has also cut funding to their perceived 'enemies', or areas of community interest which are not aligned to their political interests. For example, $534 million has been cut from national Indigenous programs, with threats to cut a further $600 million[5] and the cutback of $140,000 of funding to the Refugee Council of Australia.

And finally, the Minister for Women is actually a man—Tony Abbott. Shades of Saudi Arabia and the Taliban.

So, will this silent coup succeed? Although the next federal election is not due until 2016, Tony Abbott is fast becoming the Achilles' heel of the Liberal–National Party and questions are being asked of his leadership.

While it's difficult to see how Tony Abbott would be deposed by his own party, it is interesting that after only nine months in office, there is already open discussion within the media about leadership change and, as the putative heir apparent, Malcolm Turnbull has been the focus of attention, causing ructions with the Liberal–National Coalition team.

Tony Abbott's net approval ratings are minus 30 (approval rating of 30 per cent, less disapproval rate of 60 per cent) and the Liberal–National Party is currently polling at 45 per cent on the two-party preferred vote, a level that has been consistent over the past five months. The recent Budget has been poorly received and managed in a politically incomprehensive manner. The proposed changes to higher education, introduced by

---

4   Latika Bourke, ABC News, 'Sir Peter Cosgrove sworn in as Australia's 26th Governor-General', 28 March 2014. http://www.abc.net.au/news/2014-03-28/peter-cosgrove-sworn-in-governor-general/5351436

5   Lindy Kerin, ABC News, 'Warren Mundine puts Indigenous council offside with suggestion of extra $600 million in savings to portfolio', 5 June 2014. http://www.abc.net.au/news/2014-06-05/warren-mundine-suggests-more-indigenous-programs-savings/5503446

Minister for Education, Christopher Pyne, have been a public relations disaster. The entire political strategy has been akin to a 1979 Student Representative Council battle run by psychopathic liars, charlatans and spin doctors, based on ideological pursuits, rather than an overall plan for the betterment of the country.

Although incidents such as 'winkgate'[6] (during an ABC talkback radio session with 'Gloria', a 67-year-old pensioner, Abbott winked at his host, Jon Faine, when Gloria mentioned that she had to resort to working as a phone-sex worker to make ends meet) and the disgraceful efforts at politicising the D-Day commemorations by mentioning the repeal of the carbon and mining taxes and 'open for business' rhetoric,[7] are sideshow issues and superfluous, the cumulative impact of these minor events leads to perceptions that Australia has a Prime Minister who is increasingly not competent, and not averse to crawling into any cavernous depth to score a political point.

Although the international community doesn't vote in Australian elections, Abbott is becoming a target of ridicule overseas, for example, lampooned on a US satirical news show, *Last Week Tonight*, hosted by John Oliver.[8]

There are also reports that when he was in the US for the D-Day commemorations, he refused to meet with key political and economic figures, an odd decision, considering Australia is hosting the next G20 meeting later this year.

So will there be a change in leadership? The Liberal–National Coalition only needs to look across to its opponents for answers: the Labor Party.

Cures for cancer and regular passenger trips to Jupiter will

6   Tony Wright, *Sydney Morning Herald*, 'Abbott's wink and smirk send cyberspace into a red-hot fury', 22 May 2014. http://www.smh.com.au/federal-politics/political-opinion/abbotts-wink-and-smirk-send-cyberspace-into-a-redhot-fury-20140521-38p4e.html

7   Alexandra Back, *Sydney Morning Herald*, 'Tony Abbott raises eyebrows after linking WWII D-Day memorial with policies on mining and carbon taxes', 2 June 2014. http://www.smh.com.au/federal-politics/political-news/tony-abbott-raises-eyebrows-after-linking-wwii-dday-memorial-with-policies-on-mining-and-carbon-taxes-20140602-39cuy.html

8   HBO, *Last Week Tonight with John Oliver*, 'Tony Abbott, President of the USA of Australia', via YouTube, 2 June 2014. https://youtu.be/c3IaKVmkXuk

occur way before political scholars will be able to determine why the Labor Party, not once but twice, deposed a sitting Prime Minister just several months before a general election. So, until that research comes in to suggest whether this is a good way to run politics, it's safe to assume the Liberal–National Coalition won't copy the leadership template the Labor Party created in 2010, and will not depose Tony Abbott before the 2016 general election.

But, it takes more than a poorly performing Prime Minister for a political party to unravel.

Political loyalty has become more volatile over the past two decades and, although the Liberal–National Party holds 90 of 150 federal seats, it seems that its members have left behind their calculators and forgotten that only 16 seats stand between them and another long stint on the Opposition benches. Christopher Pyne is a blustering walking media disaster. Treasurer Joe Hockey is not on top of his portfolio, often providing answers that are contradicted by party members. Assistant Treasurer, Senator Mathias Cormann, thinks that his Terminator 'I'll be back' rhetoric is a vote winner but, hard to believe, is an even greater media disaster than Christopher Pyne, culminating with the 'cigar smoking' episode on Budget eve, where Hockey and Cormann lounged on an outdoor bench at Parliament House and smoked cigars.[9]

Senator David Johnston, who not only is a poorly performing Minister for Defence but, perhaps one of the least effective ministers in recent memory, is believed to be on the way to being sacked, amongst rumours of a cabinet reshuffle[10]—after only nine months of government.

---

9   Nine News, 'Hockey and Cormann enjoy cigars ahead of Budget', 10 May 2014. http://www.9news.com.au/national/2014/05/10/12/14/treasurer-and-fm-enjoy-cigars-ahead-of-budget

10 Heath Aston & James Massola, *The Age*, 'Attacks on Malcolm Turnbull have been linked to a reshuffle of the Abbott ministry', 6 June 2014. http://www.theage.com.au/federal-politics/political-news/attacks-on-malcolm-turnbull-have-been-linked-to-a-reshuffle-of-the-abbott-ministry-20140605-39lzc.html

Generally, it seems that the six years of the time in Opposition between 2007–13 was wasted on the effort to return to government, rather than a serious attempt at policy formulation and strategies for good governance. And, in the absence of good policy formulation, the focus for the Liberal–National Party will always be about preservation and maintaining government, irrespective of how poorly its policies (such as the Budget) are received. And what will this result in? The same features as the military *junta*.

So, a silent coup is taking place, but it won't succeed. It will take a while for the damage to be unraveled but it is hoped the silent coup will be repelled in 2016, if not before.

*

What is Tony Abbott hiding?

7 September 2014

There's a rather odd case that's developing in the media and it's the question of whether the Prime Minister, Tony Abbott, is fit to hold office in the Australian Parliament. Before you start thinking, 'Oh no, not another critique on Tony Abbott's character', this is more to do with a technicality and nothing to do with his moral character (although that's one thing that we'll end up on).

According to Section 44 of the Australian Constitution,[1] a person who is a subject or a citizen or entitled to the rights or privileges of a subject or citizen of a foreign power, is disqualified from becoming a candidate for election to the Australian Parliament. This has been widely interpreted to mean that persons with dual citizenship are not permitted to stand for election.

Tony Abbott was born in the United Kingdom in 1957, and arrived in Australia with his parents in 1960. His father is British and his mother is Australian. Although living in Australia for most of his life, he did not become an Australian citizen until 1981, a requirement for his Rhodes scholarship.

There has been conjecture for some time as to whether Tony

---

1   Wikpedia, 'Section 44 of the Constitution of Australia', http://en.wikipedia.org/wiki/Section_44_of_the_Constitution_of_Australia

Abbott renounced his British citizenship before he entered federal Parliament in 1994, but the issue has developed further over the past month, with the investigations by Tony Magrathea, detailing his attempts to determine whether this renunciation ever occurred.[2]

This seems to be such a small (but important) matter, and it's peculiar that Tony Abbott's chief-of-staff, Peta Credlin, has gone to great lengths to refuse Freedom of Information requests for access to documentation from the National Archives of Australia, or the British Office of Records.

It seems that there are three possibilities for what might have occurred:

Option 1: Tony Abbott renounced his British citizenship before 1994. Tony Abbott might have renounced his British citizenship, as required by the Australian Constitution, before seeking election in early 1994. If this is the case, to stop this issue spiralling out of control and continuing to be a minor irritant, Tony Abbott should release documentation showing that he formally renounced his British citizenship.

Option 2: Tony Abbott renounced his British citizenship after 1994. If this is the case, it's not possible to 'unelect' a person after they have completed a parliamentary term—but Section 46 of the Constitution stipulates[3] the disciplinary measure for sitting in Parliament while disqualified; the sum of £100 per day of sitting. Again, Tony Abbott should release any documentation, pay any disciplinary fines (accumulated at the appropriate Commonwealth Bonds rate), and work out a way of explaining this to the Australian public. This would be an embarrassment, but with two years before the next federal election, a minor irritant would be removed.

....

2   Tony Magrathea, 'Asking about Abbott's dual nationality', 10 December 2014. http://
    tonymagrathea.blogspot.com.au/2014/12/a-letter-to-police-and-justice.html
3   Australian Politics, 'Australian Constitution – Section 46 – Penalty for sitting when
    disqualified'. http://australianpolitics.com/text/46.shtml

Option 3: Tony Abbott has never renounced his British citizenship. If Tony Abbott has *not* renounced his British citizenship, he would be disqualified from Parliament. A by-election in the seat of Warringah would be called and he would need to be re-elected to resume his seat. I would imagine that the Liberal Party would call the by-election urgently—there are no set times for how soon a by-election can be held—the most immediate by-election was for the seat of East Sydney in 1903, held 17 days after it was declared vacant. Under this scenario, we would have another Prime Minister, probably the current Treasurer, Joe Hockey (although, who knows what kind of a result a Liberal Party room ballot would throw up).

The precedents for this latter possibility are clear. Jackie Kelly, a Minister in the Howard government, was elected to Parliament during the general election of 1996 but, after a challenge by the Labor Party on the basis of her citizenship status and employment by the Crown, her election was declared invalid and a by-election was held.[4] After she renounced her New Zealand citizenship and terminated her employment with the RAAF, she won that by-election with an even greater margin, but the point is that her initial candidacy was declared invalid. The One Nation candidate in the Senate, Heather Hill, was also ruled ineligible after the 1998 general election.[5]

In this situation, Tony Abbott could not survive. Aside from the ignominy, a Prime Minister who scorns asylum seekers for throwing away their documentation and demands that the unemployed should document two job applications every day, can't even get his own house in order and ensure that his candidacy in the Parliament is legal? The Labor Party would have a field day.

....

4   Australian Electoral Commission, 'Lindsay by-election, 1996': http://www.aec.gov.au/Elections/supplementary_by_elections/Lindsay.htm

5   High Court of Australia, *Sue v Hill* [1999] HCA 30; 199 CLR 462; 163 ALR 648; 73 ALJR 1016 (23 June 1999). http://www.austlii.edu.au/au/cases/cth/HCA/1999/30.html

While many broken promises have been brushed away by the Prime Minister and truth-stretching has become the norm for this government, this is not a situation that can be easily flicked away, or explained in half-truths and blatant lies. It would entrench the idea in the electorate that there is one rule for some, and another rule for others or, in this case, a rule not even properly adhered to. It would also go to the heart of competency.

Ultimately, it might not matter to the Australian public. But, the Australian Constitution is an important document and the rules are there for all to see. The laws and sections of the Constitution are either important, or they are not, and as Tony Abbott claims to be a firm believer in constitutional law, he'd be the first one to recognise this.

The office of the Prime Minister is going to great lengths to withhold information about whether Tony Abbott has renounced his British citizenship. It would be better for the Prime Minister to release any documentation that is relevant to this, and clear up this matter of public importance.

*

ABC fails the test of good journalism

14 October 2014

For pure televisual theatre, it's hard to go past last week's episode of *Lateline*, where the program's host, Emma Alberici locked horns with prominent Sydney member of Hizb ut-Tahrir, Wassim Doureihi.[1] But that's pretty much what it was—theatre—and a political stitch up on an easy political target.

As far as journalistic standards are concerned, it was probably the worst piece of television journalism I've ever witnessed, and certainly the least impressive on the 21 years of *Lateline*. If I want to watch boxing, I'll go to a boxing match, or watch a polemicist like Bill O'Reilly on Fox News.

But I don't expect to see the lowest of low journalism on *Lateline*, where we end up knowing less than when we started (in case you are interested in some more informed discussion about the Caliphate, or to get a better understanding of what Doureihi was trying to discuss before being rudely interrupted by Alberici, listen to Radio National's excellent documentary, 'Dreaming of the Caliphate'[2]).

---

1 *Lateline*, ABC, 'IS a reaction to unjust occupation', 8 October 2014. http://www.abc.net.au/lateline/content/2014/s4103227.htm
2 *Encounter*, ABC Radio National, 'Dreaming of the Caliphate', 11 October 2014. http://www.abc.net.au/radionational/programs/encounter/dreaming-of-the-caliphate/5795320

If you haven't heard, Hizb ut-Tahrir is one of the more radical Islamic groups which has the goal of uniting Muslim countries into a caliphate ruled by Islamic law. Well, this certainly isn't something that I'd be pushing for but, if it's alright for Jewish people to create a homeland in Israel over historic lands, surely it must be alright for Islamic people to re-create the Caliphate over their historic lands too?

Hizb ut-Tahrir has existed since 1953 and the organisation has been banned in Russia, Pakistan, Bangladesh and Germany. It has a branch in Australia[3] and Wassim Doureihi is one of its prominent members. Australia attempted a ban on the group in 2005 but, after the organisation received clearance from ASIO, the ban was rejected by the Australian Government.

Alberici had invited Doureihi on the program on the pretext of helping 'Australians better understand what it is that you stand for' but then immediately followed this up with the obligatory question asked of all Muslim leaders in the media—whether he supported 'the murderous campaign being waged by Islamic State fighters in Iraq'.

Doureihi wanted to step back to provide a context for why Islamic State exists (which is why he was invited onto the program) and the events in the Middle East, including a century of colonial occupation and oppression, the Gulf War in 1991 and the invasion of Iraq in 2003 which in my opinion, along with the events in Syria over the past five years and the endemic corruption in Egypt that have been aided and abetted by the West since 1981, have created the vacuum for Islamic State to exist.

Maybe it's just me, but I would have preferred to listen to Doureihi argue his points and outline the reasons why Islamic State exists, rather than being berated by a political novice for not answering the question in a manner that she wanted him to. A more experienced interviewer, rather than

3   Hizb ut-Tahrir Australia, http://www.hizb-australia.org

showing exasperation and unprofessional emotion, might have considered other ways to ask the question to arrive at the answer she was seeking, rather than shouting the same question again and again, and abusing her guest.

But, in this continuous age of The War on Terror, that might be too sensible—Doureihi was easy pickings and ever since the Prime Minister, Tony Abbott mused on 2GB Radio in early 2014, that 'a lot of people feel at the moment that the ABC instinctively takes everyone's side but Australia's',[4] there's no doubt the ABC has been trying to get back onto Team Australia. And the following day after the interview, Abbott declared that 'she's [Alberici] a feisty interviewer... good on her for having a go and I think she spoke for our country last night'. I can imagine ABC management would have been doing a round of high-fives in their offices that afternoon—suddenly, they're back in favour with the Australian Government, part of Team Australia again and the future of *Lateline* will be guaranteed. If the reputation of Wassim Doureihi was massacred through a political hatchet job and a set up, well, that's just collateral damage.

And for some bizarre reason, possibly to show Australians what a 'good Muslim' looks like, the following night, *Lateline* invited Haset Sali, a former president of the Australian Federation of Islamic Councils, to discuss his interpretations of the Koran.[5] Now, if the interview with Doureihi was dynamic televisual theatre, this was quite the opposite, akin to watching a old toothless tiger at the zoo, going through its paces, responding to perfunctory questions.

And if all of this wasn't bad enough, we had the spectacle of congratulations through other mainstream media, most notably at the *Sydney Morning Herald*.[6] It was almost like an 'our

---

4   Latika Bourke, ABC News, 'Prime Minister Tony Abbott says ABC not on Australia's side in interview with 2GB', 4 February 2014. http://www.abc.net.au/news/2014-01-29/tony-abbott-steps-up-criticism-of-abc/5224676

5   *Lateline*, ABC, 'Koran does not advocate a Caliphate', 9 October 2014. http://www.abc.net.au/lateline/content/2014/s4104089.htm

6   Latika Bourke, *Sydney Morning Herald*, 'Tony Abbott backs Lateline host Emma Alberici

girl does good' type of reporting, as if someone had just scored big, somewhere on the big stage. It wasn't quite cultural cringe, but it was close.

Now, don't get me wrong—Emma Alberici is a good television presenter and journalist but not well suited to a political program such as *Lateline* that frequently deals with international issues—she has great expertise in business reporting and would be better suited to this area. She was well out of her depth during the Israeli bombing of Gaza in July 2014—compare the interviewing of Mustafa Barghouti the leader of the Palestinian National Initiative[7] with Dore Gold, Senior Foreign Policy Advisor to the Israeli Government.[8] The two interviews are like chalk and cheese; Barghouti interviewed as though the Palestinians are the ones dropping the bombs, with constant hectoring and interjections—I was quite surprised Barghouti didn't storm off the set—Gold given a free reign as though he's the purest person in the Middle East and nothing to answer for.

So, what can the ABC do? The government is the one that pays their bills, so it's more sensible to keep them onside, whether it's by providing the so-called 'balance' on programs such as *Insiders*, and *7.30*, or by harassing a Muslim spokesperson on *Lateline* and dove-tailing into the government's agenda.

Media institutions are going through difficult transitions, and the ABC is no exception, with the changing media landscape and the entropic nature of diverse medias. But where are the good journalists? The problems started with the introduction of public relations and advertising streams into journalism courses in the late 1980s, where spin doctoring and media management to suit corporate diktats became more critical than protecting

---

over fiery Hizb ut-Tahrir interview', 9 October 2014. http://www.smh.com.au/federal-politics/political-news/tony-abbott-backs-lateline-host-emma-alberici-over-fiery-hizb-uttahrir-interview-20141009-113fxd.html

7   *Lateline*, ABC, 'Massacres must stop', 29 July 2014. http://www.abc.net.au/lateline/content/2014/s4056773.htm

8   *Lateline*, ABC, 'Israel shouldn't feel guilty for protecting citizens', 30 July 2014. http://www.abc.net.au/lateline/content/2014/s4057586.htm

the public good and the public interest.

And now, we're seeing the results—very few political journalists of repute and most who can't understand the difference between appeasing their corporate master (whether that be the ABC, or News Limited) and matters that relate to the public interest and informing the community, as well as feeling that their professional careers depend on finding the next scoop—or humiliating the nearest radical Muslim leader.

Since the Australian Federal Police raids in Brisbane, Sydney and Melbourne in early September, the media has performed badly, reporting half-facts and outright lies, duly reporting any rubbish put out by the authorities without bothering to check the veracity. The sad point is that this type of propaganda management is bad enough in countries with state-controlled media but Australia is a supposedly free society where journalists are free to report matters as they see fit, without threats of jail or court action (although that may change soon, with the Australian Government passing draconian legislation[9] to allow journalists to be incarcerated for up to 10 years).

So, the performance of *Lateline* is just another chapter in the recent drop in standards of journalism. Should we expect better? Yes, we should, but in the new age of The War of Terror, maybe it's a tall order.

*

9   Naomi Woodley, ABC News, 'Senate passes new counter-terrorism laws giving stronger powers to intelligence agency ASIO', 26 September 2014. http://www.abc.net.au/news/2014-09-25/new-counter-terrorism-laws-pass-the-senate/5770256

Tony Abbott: On his way out of office

8 December 2014

And so ends another parliamentary year in Canberra. While it doesn't feel like the year has had the same level of high drama and tension as 2012 or for most of 2013, it has been unique in many ways.

A first-term government is seriously being considered as a first-term loser (not since James Scullin lost office in 1931 has there been a one-term federal government) and it hasn't even reached its mid-way point.

The Treasurer, Joe Hockey, is rumoured to be on the verge of being replaced by the Minister for Communications, Malcolm Turnbull, and there is also now open speculation about Tony Abbott being replaced as Prime Minister before the next election. These are speculations that are usually reserved for parties in Opposition, or long-term governments, not a first-term government elected in a landslide victory after several years of leadership instability in the Labor Party and a hung Parliament.

So, what's behind this speculation, and is the Liberal–National government performing as badly as its poll numbers suggest? The most obvious point is that Tony Abbott has never been widely regarded by the electorate, even after he assumed the position of Prime Minister—his approval numbers are usually in negative territory (approval, minus disapproval rating).

But there are other factors in play, most notably the introduction of several extreme pieces of legislation that were never discussed during the 2013 election campaign—the reforms to higher education, the attempt to repeal funding for Labor's Gonski school education reforms, the proposed Medicare $7 co-payment tax, raising taxes and cutting pensions. On top of this, the Liberal–National Coalition has implemented $308 million of cuts to the ABC and SBS over five years, even though Tony Abbott emphatically stated that this would not occur if he won the election.

Then there have been other strange actions, such as the $250 million for a modified chaplains program, which excludes secular workers, and the $821 million over the next four years to fund training for priests. Aside from the state–church separation issues, in the context of the so-called 'Budget emergency' the Coalition has been claiming since it won office, this is an outrageously high figure for what is, essentially a Tony Abbott pet project (remembering that Abbott trained as a seminarian for two years, and has strong relationships with figures in the Catholic church, most notably, George Pell).

From the time Tony Abbott became leader of the Coalition in 2009, he performed the very effective political campaign to remove Kevin Rudd and Julia Gillard, and then to win the election in 2013. But, the political strategy employed at that time excluded a policy strategy, and this emphasis on politics only is the main reason why the Coalition currently is suffering so badly.

For all of the six years in Opposition, the Coalition primarily focused on creating chaos within Parliament, and very little else. It is surprising that Christopher Pyne has held the education portfolio since 2008—surprising in the sense that no policy of note has been released from this time (except for backgrounding about more autonomy for schools and principals). Even more surprising is the idea that Pyne expected that he could go back on his word about the funding of Labor's Gonski reforms, refashion the national curriculum into a conservative wishlist using his hand-picked right-wing colleagues (including the unfortunate Professor Barry Spurr from the University of Sydney, who referred to people in racist emails as "abos", "bogans", "fatsoes", "Mussies" and "Chinky-Poos"—perhaps not the right type of person to be preparing a curriculum for school children), and introduce a massive deregulation of the higher education sector, without causing great consternation within the community and media backlash.

Certainly, if these policy ideas were presented to the public *prior* to the election, and the public voted for it, then the democratic course of action allows for the implementation of such a program. But, that never happened. And it's obvious from the reaction of the public, the agenda is something that the public would never vote for.

The Medicare co-payment tax is something that was inarticulately announced by Minister for Health, Peter Dutton, in December 2013, several months *after* the election. It's bizarre to think that Dutton was considered Liberal leadership material in 2007, because his performance as Minister has been mediocre. The Medicare co-payment tax has been promoted as a mechanism to 'price signal' visits to the doctor, making the Medicare system sustainable in the future (why it is 'unsustainable' now has never fully been discussed), linked to a medical research fund of $20 billion, or a way to reduce the Budget deficit.

The problem with this reasoning is a Medicare co-payment tax can either be linked to a medical research fund *or* it can be used to reduce the Budget deficit: it can't do both. 'Price signalling' to reduce visits to the doctor means that people will become sick more often, and more chronically, adding to future Budget costs by increasing hospital medical expenses in later years. The public has recognised this incoherency and understood the flaws in what the Coalition is attempting to do.

In his most recent press conference, Tony Abbott announced that 2014 for the Coalition was a year of "very considerable achievement", where the government had shown "considerable courage and strength of character", often referring to "stopping the boats" (as if that's an issue that puts food on the table of working families), "reducing the debt" (the government has actually increased debt by $4.9 billion), and "removing the carbon and mining taxes" (carbon emissions have increased since the carbon tax was removed; the mining tax, according to the Coalition's own words, wasn't raising any revenue anyway— so the decision is a future gift to the mining industry when their profits reach a 'super' level again).

Abbott has also claimed the success of free trade agreements with China,[1] Japan[2] and South Korea,[3] but these have been developed by successive governments over many years— understandably, the government that signs the agreement takes the political credit, but it was primarily the work of the Howard, Rudd and Gillard governments.

While Abbott is keen to promote this idea of "very considerable achievement", the record shows nothing of the sort. The May Budget still has key measures that have not been passed by the Senate, and many other projects that have been attempted by the Coalition are driven by ideological desires, personal prejudices devoid of any supporting research. Ministers have been very ineffective and error prone (choose from any of this list: Kevin Andrews, David Johnston, Joe Hockey, Christopher Pyne, George Brandis, Peter Dutton,

---

1   Department of Foreign Affairs and Trade, China–Australia Free Trade Agreement. http://dfat.gov.au/trade/agreements/chafta/pages/australia-china-fta.aspx

2   Department of Foreign Affairs and Trade, Japan–Australia Economic Partnership Agreement. http://dfat.gov.au/trade/agreements/jaepa/pages/japan-australia-economic-partnership-agreement.aspx

3   Department of Foreign Affairs and Trade, Korea–Australia Free Trade Agreement. http://dfat.gov.au/trade/agreements/kafta/pages/korea-australia-fta.aspx

Mathias Cormann) and have often provided contradictory public statements about their policy and political intentions.

And the main reason for this situation is the low level of policy development during their time in Opposition during 2007–13, and expending all of their energies in creating chaos for the Labor government, rather than preparing themselves for when they eventually returned to office. As a result of having few policy ideas and springing ideologically-driven surprises upon the electorate, the Abbott government is the most poorly polling first-term government ever, and by some measure. It's aggregate polling is currently 45 per cent on the two-party preferred vote, compared to Howard's 56 per cent, and Rudd's 58 per cent at the same point in the political cycle. It has been behind in all published polls over the past 12 months.

But a government and its ministry can only be as good as its Prime Minister will allow. Abbott's prime ministership has been poor, and he has been more intent on governing as a tribal leader of the Liberal party, and a narrow partisan collection of business people, spivs, rent seekers and hangers on, instead of government for the broader community—which is where the electoral rewards will be, not in some conservative mind-set that smells like the 1950s, and tries to take us back to supposed glory days that never existed.

The recent G20 meeting (the economic forum hosting the leaders and bank governors of the 20 largest world economies) in Brisbane was possibly the first time that Abbott's Coalition colleagues were genuinely starting to think: 'who is this guy'. 'What is his purpose and why is he our Prime Minister?'. His partisanship knows no bounds—denying Labor's Deputy Leader, Tanya Plibersek, access and entry to the G20 meeting— and using his opening address to the world leaders to announce his government's actions and complaining about the reaction to his proposed Medicare co-payment tax of $7.

A leader governing in the national interest would realise that it's not always about themselves, or their political party, and would include Opposition spokespeople for these occasions (yes, hard to believe for Abbott, but there will be future Labor governments that will need to negotiate with other countries in the world). They would also discuss broader economic agendas, rather than using the occasion to rescue a poor political standing and promoting partisan propaganda. Judging by their reactions, perhaps it was the world leaders that were also thinking: 'who is this guy'. 'What is his purpose and why is he *their* Prime Minister?'.

It's not so much that Abbott was an embarrassment to Australia at the G20 but, as many analysts have suggested, it was a lost opportunity to present Australian ideals and ideas to an international audience. The event itself was a success and, irrespective of the foolishness of a leader, other countries used the event to work towards consensus on global economic and climate change agendas. Australia behaved like a little country from hicksville, complaining about US President Barack Obama's speech referring to climate change, because it didn't reflect well upon their narrow perspectives. Global leaders understand host countries will use the forum for their domestic political advantage but any more performances like Abbott's, and future G20 events will be hosted via Skype and Dropbox.

Tony Abbott is the accidental Prime Minister, in a similar way that George W. Bush became the accidental US President in 2000. He only defeated Malcolm Turnbull by one vote in the Liberal leadership ballot in 2009 and had to rely on Labor Party leadership instability and a grotesquely negative campaign to become Prime Minister. He can't perform on the world stage, as the 2014 Davos address showed and the G20 performance confirmed. He is increasingly unable to perform on the national stage, and after the mainstream media overlooked many of his flaws and blunders during the first 12 months of his term, the worm has slowly started to turn.

In a recent interview on Channel 9's *Today* program, host Karl Stefanovic stated the obvious: 'no one is buying what you are selling'.[4] Abbott looked about as stunned as Romanian despot Nicolae Ceausescu on the steps of Revolution Square in Bucharest in 1989, just before being deposed and executed. Abbott has not been seriously scrutinised by the mainstream media and would have least expected such an interrogation from Chanel Nine, supposedly friends of the Liberal Party. Former fanatics and cheerleaders at News Limited have started to seriously critique Abbott's performance, perhaps hoping for a repeat of the 'mean and tricky' memo from Shane Stone[5] in April 2001, which prompted a change in John Howard's political strategy and was supposedly one of the factors behind the Coalition winning the federal election later in that year.

But Tony Abbott is not like John Howard. Just like an elite athlete, Prime Ministers need to be tried and tested, need to go the hard yards in tough interviews, develop difficult policy ideas and work out ways to implement them with broad electoral support. It's a test of their character and the electorate admire toughness and hardness in political leadership. But Abbott has had an easy ride in his path to becoming Prime Minister and soft interviews, such as last week's interview[6] on ABC's *7.30* with Leigh Sales, do him no favours. He used three-word slogans and policy lies during the 2013 election campaign to become Prime Minister, and developed little policy of any use during his time in Opposition. His signature paid parental leave policy is ridiculously expensive and favours high-income families. But, it is yet to be implemented and, judging by his demeanour, will never be implemented. It was a cynical plan to feminise Abbott's image, and hasn't achieved that goal.

He expected the electorate to accept his unannounced

4   Alex McKinnon, *Junkee*, 'Karl Stefanovic Ripped Tony Abbott To Bits On 'The Today Show' This Morning', 2 December 2014. http://junkee.com/karl-stefanovic-ripped-tony-abbott-to-bits-on-the-today-show-this-morning/46387

5   Graham Young, *On Line Opinion*, 'Mean, tricky, out of touch and not listening', 15 April 2001. http://www.onlineopinion.com.au/view.asp?article=1810

6   ABC Television, *7.30*, 'We've fundamentally honoured core commitments' says Tony Abbott', 4 December 2014. http://www.abc.net.au/7.30/content/2014/s4142593.htm

radical right wing agenda and failed to understand why anyone could question his government's motives. Australia is neither to the far left, or to the far right, and any attempts to pursue either of these extremes, especially when such an agenda has not been announced, or taken to an election, will never be accepted by the electorate.

While Tony Abbott is a radical, he's a lazy and impatient radical. Such ideas, as John Howard found out, need to be developed as long-term projects. And, as former Labor Prime Ministers Bob Hawke and Paul Keating understood in the 1980s and 1990s, the electorate needs persuasion to be attracted to new and big ideas. But, as Howard found out to his detriment in 2007, taking a radical program such as the WorkChoices program without taking it to an election first, leads to great electoral problems.

My feeling is that Tony Abbott's prime ministership is doomed, and unable to be repaired. I've previously outlined the reasons why I thought Abbott would be a dangerous leader. But, I've changed my opinion and, to paraphrase the only quote from John Maynard Keynes that Abbott will ever use, when the fact changes, I change my mind. I now believe Abbott is more in the style of an incompetent Prime Minister, behaving as though the office can be used as a play adventure zone for ideologically-driven unfinished projects, influenced by the drivel of B.A. Santamaria, and driven by payback from his unsuccessful time as student president at the University of Sydney.

Yes, Abbott is incompetent: not in the same way that Billy McMahon was incompetent in the early 1970s, but incompetent nevertheless. He'll more than likely be replaced as leader some time in 2015 and then he can continue the relationship with his Chief of Staff that won't inflict any further damage on the Australia community. But worse is to come. If Abbott goes, he might be replaced by someone who is truly dangerous and even more politically psychopathic: Prime Minister Scott Morrison.

*

Scott Morrison didn't become Prime Minister but was instrumental in securing the parliamentary numbers for Malcolm Turnbull in the challenge to Tony Abbott's leadership in September 2015. His reward? Treasurer of Australia.

The Medicare fiasco and a spiralling government

19 January 2015

There are many ways to describe the Liberal–National Party's recent fiasco on Medicare funding: unrealistic zealotry, ideological, 'own goal', 'self-inflicted wound' (I'd prefer to settle on political ineptitude) but the most important question can be reduced to one word: why?

Firstly, it must be pointed out that the Liberal–National Party has never mentioned changes to Medicare during an election campaign ever, for the main reason that it's political poison. Historically, any changes to Medicare introduced by the conservatives have always occurred early in a term, and electioneering, such as their 2013 campaign, has usually been reduced to politically innocuous statements such as 'no changes to Medicare', or the 1996 campaign, when John Howard pledged to 'retain Medicare'.

The unexpected announcement in December 2013, only several months after the Liberal–National Party assumed office, by then Minister for Health, Peter Dutton, that the government was considering a $7 Medicare co-payment was foolhardy, especially considering their election pledge of 'no changes to Medicare'. The $7 Medicare co-payment was included in

Treasurer Joe Hockey's 2014–15 Budget, again, flying in the face of their 2013 election pledge, as well as community opposition.

The plan to re-direct the $7 Medicare co-payment into a health research future fund was purely a political stance, designed to sugar-coat the measure with the electorate. Who the beneficiaries would be of this fund was never pointed out, but it would be safe to assume that those medical pharmaceutical companies close to the Liberal–National Party, such as Aspen Medical, would be the first in line to receive any research funds.

But this measure was cluttered with messaging from the government that the Medicare co-payment was necessary because of—depending on which backbencher briefed the media—'the Budget emergency', 'price signaling', or, more inventively, that the Medicare system was 'growing at a rapid and unsustainable rate'. This has been the greatest fabrication because spending on Medicare is growing in real terms but, as a proportion of GDP and tax revenue, it has actually slowed.[1]

In keeping with the desperation, in early 2014, Joe Hockey claimed that the cost of Medicare was $65 billion per year, when its actual cost is $19 billion per year. So, was the Medicare co-payment about supporting a health research fund (open to cronyism), spiralling costs (found to be not actually true), or a revenue raising measure to reduce debt? Well, it seems like none of the above: irrespective of what they might say (and sometimes, all matter of different ideas in unison), the Liberal–National Party are implacably opposed to Medicare. Always have been, always will be.

Facing community opposition and a Senate that refused to acquiesce, Dutton pulled the legislation in October 2014, but then proceeded with a $5 reduction in Medicare payments to doctors, a reduction to be made up by the patient, and at the discretion of the doctor. While this measure only needed

---

1 Glen Murray, 'Medicare's growth isn't out of control – It's actually slowing', 16 January 2015. http://www.glennmurray.com.au/medicares-growth-isnt-out-of-control-its-actually-slowing

government regulation, rather than legislation, the Senate could easily reverse this change.

While this is more or less fitting into the Coalition's desire for 'price signaling', a bizarre concept when applied to health, especially when encouraging people to access medical care now acts as a strong preventative health measure and saves the health budget $4 billion per year,[2] nothing was quite as coming out of left field as the idea of reducing of Medicare payments to doctors by $20.10 for consultations lasting less than 10 minutes.

This plan was announced in early January 2015, for introduction on 19 January: one week for medical centres and doctors to re-work their budgets and implement this plan within their practices. Again, dispersed media messages were offered: the old one of 'making Medicare sustainable', 'price signaling', 'making doctors spend more time with their patients' (all seemingly contradictory statements—we can't encourage doctors to spend more time with their patient, which will cost the government more, and claim that it will save money) and the idea of 'eliminating six-minute medicine', even though six-minute medicine is another myth that has been debunked comprehensively.[3]

Why Tony Abbott decided to pick a fight with the Australian Medical Association (a doctor's union that has created many Liberal–National Party supporters and political aspirants, such as Brendan Nelson, Bill Glasson and Rosanna Capolingua) and rail against a profession that is highly respected by the Australian community, remains a mystery (86 per cent rate doctors 'very highly', according to Roy Morgan's Image of Annual Professions Survey.[4] Incidentally, federal politicians are

2   Department of Health, *A Healthier Future for All Australians: National Health and Hospitals Reform Commission* – Final Report June 2009. http://www.health.gov.au/internet/main/publishing.nsf/content/nhhrc-report

3   Amanda Davey, *6 Minutes of Interesting Stuff For Doctors*, 'Six-minute medicine: debunking the myth', 17 June 2014. http://www.6minutes.com.au/blogs/6minutes-insight/six-minute-medicine-is-just-a-myth

4   Roy Morgan Research, 'Roy Morgan Image of Professions Survey 2014 – Nurses still most highly regarded – followed by Doctors, Pharmacists & High Court

rated 23 per cent, or number 26 on the list of 30).

It's also evident that the regulation to cut Medicare payments would have been overturned by the Senate, so it is unclear why Abbott decided to persist with and defend the highly unpopular proposal. Less than 24 hours after Abbott was spending his political capital like a banker with other peoples' money and defending the planned proposal,[5] new Minister for Health, Sussan Ley, dumped the proposal on 15 January, four days before it was to be implemented. But, like gluttons for punishment, Ley announced that the backdown was because of being "deeply concerned by the misinformation that is causing confusion for patients and confusion for doctors", ignoring the fact that her government caused the confusion in the first place, but then reiterating the government remained committed to a GP co-payment as a price signal in the health system.

Sussan Ley cut short a cruise holiday to make the announcement—why a newly-anointed Minister for Health would decide to go on a cruise holiday when a very likely political storm was brewing is unclear—it shows more political incompetence and a government that prefers holidaying rather than hard policy work. Sure, Ministers are entitled to holidays but, if I became Minister for Health, I'd cancel holidays and swat up on my new portfolio. Joe Hockey also seems to have been on extended holidays, although he was in the media recently announcing yet another reason for the Medicare co-payment: that soon we'll be living to age of 150,[6] and should be expected to contribute more to personal health care.

Judges', 11 April 2014. http://www.roymorgan.com/findings/5531-image-of-professions-2014-201404110537

5   Latika Bourke, *Sydney Morning Herald*, 'Tony Abbott defends $20 cut to Medicare rebate for short visits to the doctor', 14 January 2015. http://www.smh.com.au/federal-politics/political-news/tony-abbott-defends-20-cut-to-medicare-rebate-for-short-visits-to-the-doctor-20150114-12nqs3.html

6   Matthew Knott, *Sydney Morning Herald*, 'Joe Hockey raises prospect of Australians living until 150 to justify budget cuts', 19 January 2015. http://www.smh.com.au/federal-politics/political-news/joe-hockey-raises-prospect-of-australians-living-until-150-to-justify-budget-cuts-20150119-12t3m1.html

So, after a disastrous few weeks to commence 2015—a year that Tony Abbott promised to 'reset' his government and start off afresh with better performance—we're back to square one. There is no policy on Medicare fees, co-payments or rebates, except that the government will undertake "wide-ranging" consultation with doctors and the community across the country to come with "sensible options" for Medicare reform, and still remains committed to 'price signaling'. All in the context of the Liberal–National Party facing a challenging state election in Queensland on 31 January.

This is after six years in Opposition between 2007–2013—ample time to carry out the wide-ranging consultations with doctors and the community, in the search of "sensible options"—and 15 months in government. There's no clear policy, no clear understanding of what they hope to achieve, except for radical and mindless cost-cutting measures which will eventually benefit private health funds, and cost the public more over the long term.

Policy on the run, multiple and contradictory messages, lack of thought-out programs, are all the issues that Tony Abbott complained about when the Labor Party was in office, and gained great political traction in doing so. Sure, there was a great deal of ambiguity in Labor's messaging but many good public policy ideas had their genesis at the Australia 2020 Summit[7] in 2008, four months after Labor was elected.

Compare this with the Liberal–National Party performance since their election in September 2013, where ideas are based on prejudice and ideological pursuits in education, health, immigration, energy, welfare, taxation and finance, and influenced by the spivs and rent seekers such as business people Tony Shepherd and Maurice Newman, and the conservative think-tank, the Institute of Public Affairs. Check the list of regressive ideas from the Institute of Public Affairs and see how

7   Australia Policy Online, Australia 2020 Summit: final report, 2 June 2008. http://apo.
    org.au/node/15061

many have been implemented by the Liberal–National Party:

1. 'Be like Gough: 75 radical ideas to transform Australia'[8] (which includes almost every possible permutation of reactionary thought and destruction of the state)
2. 25 more ideas for Tony Abbott[9] (in case the original list of 75 reactionary ideas were not severe enough).

It's clear that these are the ideas that are more in tune with the American Tea Party movement[10] and based on an anti-intellectual right-wing libertarian perspective that is too unpalatable for Australia. But it's the direction that Tony Abbott wants to take us towards.

However, Tony Abbott is not the only problem—it's the reactionary conservative ideas embedded within the Liberal–National Party. It's like a combination of a dominating lazy stingy right-wing conservative ideologues and *laissez-faire* free-marketeers—all within the same party. Tony Abbott and the LNP wasted their time in Opposition, and now they're wasting ours. Ministers go on extended holidays while the country withers away, meaning that we have ludicrous and ill-thought-out policy changes that are thought up like brain musings that explode into the ether within days of being announced.

It's no way to run a government. Three-word slogans worked well for Tony Abbott in Opposition, but hard work is required in government to prosecute a case and take the public along the journey.

A proposal for a $3.50 Medicare co-payment in 1991 was the beginning of the end for Bob Hawke as Prime Minister: he was out of the job within five months. Tony Abbott is facing the same demise. It could sooner, it could be later, but either

8   John Roskam, James Paterson & Chris Berg, Institute of Public Affairs, 'Be like Gough: 75 radical ideas to transform Australia', https://www.ipa.org.au/publications-ipa/ipa-review-articles/be-like-gough-75-radical-ideas-to-transform-australia
9   John Roskam, James Paterson & Chris Berg, Institute of Public Affairs, '25 more ideas for Tony Abbott'. https://ipa.org.au/publications/2110/25-more-ideas-for-tony-abbott
10   Tea Party, 'About Us', http://www.teaparty.org/about-us/

way, it can't continue like this for much longer. Then it will be up to someone in the Liberal–National Party to explain how a government had lost its way, or never quite found it.

*

An Australia Day mistake

26 January 2015

Just when you thought it couldn't get any worse for the Prime Minister Tony Abbott, he makes the bizarre decision to award Prince Philip, the Duke of Edinburgh, a knighthood on Australia Day. He may have got away with it on any other day of the year, but not on Australia Day.

Sir Prince Duke Philip (amongst a long list of other unwarranted titles,[1] as well as being a Nazi sympathiser[2]). A 93-year-old symbol of old English royalty, aristocracy and establishment, prone to ludicrous gags and comments in all sorts of inappropriate situations,[3] if you like, the embodiment of a foolish casual racist.

If this was crazy–brave, it could be a decision that could be commended. But it's not brave, and it's gone beyond the realm of 'crazy'. It's something else: hubris, arrogance, haughtiness... it's in a zone of its own, a realm which has no description.

---

1   Megan Levy, *Sydney Morning Herald*, 'Prince Philip adds Australian knighthood to list of colourful titles', 26 January 2015. http://www.smh.com.au/federal-politics/political-news/prince-philip-adds-australian-knighthood-to-list-of-colourful-titles-20150126-12y3w2.html

2   Scott Thompson, *The Nazi Roots Of... The House Of Windsor*, 25 August 1997.http://www.bibliotecapleyades.net/sociopolitica/esp_sociopol_blacknobil09.htm

3   *Sydney Morning Herald*, 'Arise Prince Philip: a look at the British consort's notorious gaffes', 26 January 2015. http://www.smh.com.au/federal-politics/political-news/arise-prince-philip-a-look-at-the-british-consorts-notorious-gaffes-20150125-12y0ak.html

This is an insight into Abbott's inner thinking—it's a level of pettiness that acts as payback to all his detractors going back all the way to his time as President of the Student Representative Council at University of Sydney in 1979—an insight into his style of thinking: not so much as a 'contemporary' conservative but a conservative from the days of Empire, Menzies, Churchill, the old-school ties of Eton, smoke-fills halls of establishment, rowing boats, old money, racism, sexism, long moustaches and Windsor Castle. Sure, these are clichéd caricatures, but not that far from the aura that Abbott seems to want to promote of himself: a befuddled *ye olde world* flâneur that is lost in the modern world, can't see an independent vision of Australia and, like Robert Menzies and John Howard before him, needs to cling onto a figment of an Australia that changed many decades ago and possibly never even existed.

For me, Australia Day on 26 January is waste of a day: I usually hide out in my backyard to escape the patriotic jingoism that ruins this day. I accept that it's a great day for a new batch of Australian people that are officially recognised at citizenship ceremonies all around the country. But, it's tainted as the invasion day from 1788 that commenced a series of largely unrecognised wars and diseases that decimated the Indigenous population—where are the war memorials to let people know that many Aboriginals were killed defending their lands on the eastern seaboard and the western front?

Australia Day is currently 26 January and will probably exist at this location for some time. Whatever the merits or failings of Australia Day are, it exists as a day to recognise the many people that have carried out work in the community that strengthens the country. Following on from Adam Goodes in 2014, Rose Batty is a worthy recipient of the Australian of the Year award for 2015.[4] Many people have been recognised[5] for their work in the community over the years.

But this has been overshadowed by Tony Abbott's self-centred and indulgent idea, re-introducing imperial honours in 2014, and then awarding a outdated honour to a outdated person—a person whose family supported the Nazi regime[6] during World War II. It has taken all the attention from Australia Day as an event and continued the scorn and ridicule of Tony Abbott as a leader, and as Prime Minister.

This follows on from the Medicare fiasco over the past few weeks and the spectacle of Abbott announcing in late 2014 that he was 'resetting' his government, and changing key positions within the office of Prime Minister and Cabinet.

As Leader of the Opposition, Tony Abbott trashed the office of Prime Minister by constantly demeaning Julia Gillard, supported by his right-wing cronies at News Limited, and *The Australian*. The trashing continues, but this is all of his own work: people are openly laughing and the media is scornful of the Prime Minister's decision. Analysts are trying to work out what Abbott's political game plan is, because none of this makes any sense... unless Abbott is totally oblivious to his own failings.

Federal Parliament returns on 9 February. What Abbott's parliamentary colleagues make of his misdemeanours is anyone's guess, but expect to see some action during this week. Abbott has warned the federal Liberal–National Party to dismiss leadership speculation and not change leaders.[7] But, if they are to maintain any credibility, they'll ignore this warning and call a

4   ABC News, 'Rosie Batty, Australian of the Year, will save lives of family violence victims, former police commissioner Ken Lay says', 26 January 2015. http://www.abc.net.au/news/2015-01-26/australian-of-the-year-rosie-batty-will-save-lives-ken-lay-says/6046184

5   Australia Day 2015 Honours List. http://www.gg.gov.au/australia-day-2015-honours-list

6   Kurt Nimmo, Centre For Research on Globalization, 'The British Royal Family Supported Hitler and the Nazis', 22 May 2014. http://www.globalresearch.ca/the-british-royal-family-supported-hitler-and-the-nazis/5383589

7   *The Australian*, 'Abbott dismisses leadership rumours as 'absolute nonsense'', 22 January 2015. http://www.weeklytimesnow.com.au/news/politics/abbott-dismisses-leadership-rumours-as-absolute-nonsense/news-story/d726e027962c338a2adb4a7c72de9b7b

spill of the leadership. Insiders are expecting a challenge and I also expect to see one too.

*

Goodbye Newman, Abbott will be next

31 January 2015

State elections around Australia, especially for a first-term government seeking re-election, are usually stale stolid events. Quite often, the results offer some pointers for the federal government but, as the political operatives love to say, they are 'fought on state issues'.

But not this Queensland election. There has been an unusual synchronicity between Queensland and federal politics, with the respective leaders, Premier Campbell Newman and Prime Minister Tony Abbott, facing many leadership issues and following similar 'crash through or crash' strategies, and largely alienating the electorate with similar political agendas: public sector job cutting, austerity measures and asset sales.

Queensland Premier Campbell Newman is widely tipped to lose his seat of Ashgrove and the Liberal–National Party is expected to suffer a 10 per cent swing against it, enough to put the Labor Party within striking distance of an unlikely election victory or, at least, a much better position to be able to win the Queensland election in 2018.

Of course, governments are elected to manage budgets and ensure the security of the state, but electorates do not expect them to implement large-scale job cuts, close down schools (up to 55 closures were recommended by the Newman government[1]), enable massive and unviable destructive mining projects in environmentally sensitive zones (also offering $1.9 billion of government funds[2] for these unviable projects), or create politically motivated legislation that curtails the rights of specific groups and bikies (VLAD[3]). Perhaps too many episodes of the US television bikie series, *Sons Of Anarchy*.

Both Newman and Abbott are weak leaders that were catapulted into strong electorate positions, but have largely squandered their opportunities. Newman is a novice leader who was in the unusual position of entering the Queensland Parliament as Premier—and, if the polls are correct—will leave Parliament as Premier, unless another Liberal–National member of Parliament offers their seat to him. Abbott is in a category alone, confusing the office of Prime Minister with his own personal indulgences and political pet projects and, because of his leadership weakness, is subject to renewed leadership speculation about challenges from Malcolm Turnbull or Julie Bishop.

Weak leaders are the ones who constantly needing to talk about being 'strong' (Campbell Newman mentioned the word 'strong' 18 times in the first three minutes of his election campaign launch) or, in Abbott's case, the 'captain's call'. Repetition is the trademark of the politician, but there has to be an element of truth or electoral acceptance for this to be valued. Simply repeating 'strength' doesn't lead to the perception of

1   Alison Sandy & Tanya Chilcott, *The Courier Mail*, 'Queensland Government scheme to close 'unviable' schools could see sell-off completed in less than a year', 29 April 2013. http://www.couriermail.com.au/news/queensland/government-scheme-to-close-schools-could-see-sell-off-completed-in-less-than-a-year/story-e6freoof-1226631164556

2   Vicky Validakis, *Australian Mining*, 'Queensland government to help fund Galilee coal mines', 17 November 2014. http://www.miningaustralia.com.au/news/queensland-government-to-help-fund-galilee-coal-mi

3   ABC Radio National, *Background Briefing*, 'VLAD the bikie jailer', 2 February 2014. http://www.abc.net.au/radionational/programs/backgroundbriefing/2014-02-02/5225444

strength, if the strength is not there in the first place.

Former Prime Minister, Julia Gillard, suffered the same syndrome when she mentioned 'moving forward' 23 times in her election announcement in 2010. There is an art to repetition in politics, but in these cases, the repetition simply devalued the content, and no-one believed it anyway.

On top of these leadership and performance issues are the return of Bjelke-Peterson-style corruption, and the 'white shoe brigade'. There are allegations of corrupt behaviour[4] by Mermaid Bay MP, Ray Stevens, where he stands to make great personal gains in Gold Coast developments (Stevens refused to answer any questions about these developments and was involved in the infamous 'chicken dance' interview[5] with journalist David Donovan, where he performed a five-second chicken dance when he was stumped for answers to Donovan's questions). And in September 2014, the Newman government reduced rights that allow stakeholders to lodge appeals against mining applications,[6] without any parliamentary discussion.

Whatever the final result might be on Saturday night, there will be a massive swing against the Liberal–National Party, some polls predicting as much as 12 per cent. The repercussions for Tony Abbott will also swing with the turning tide in Queensland—Abbott and Newman are of the same leadership ilk, and the result will offer pointers for what will happen to Tony Abbott and his leadership when federal Parliament reconvenes on 9 February.

*

4   David Donovan, *Independent Australia*, 'Here we Joh again! The GC Skyride and The Integrity of Mermaid Ray', 22 December 2014. https://independentaustralia.net/politics/politics-display/skyride-and-the-integrity-of-mermaid-ray,7216

5   'Rude Mermaid Ray Stevens MP implodes over Cableway questions' via YouTube, 20 January 2015. https://youtu.be/093UhTuZmPA

6   Eric Tlozek, ABC News, 'New Queensland laws change how some stakeholders fight mining applications', 10 September 2014. http://www.abc.net.au/news/2014-09-10/mining-laws-in-queensland-will-lock-out-anti-mining-groups/5732046

The Liberal–National Party suffered a 14.0 two-party preferred swing against it at the Queensland election and it was one of those rare occasions where a government failed to secure a second term of office. The Labor Party only held nine seats prior to the election (the LNP held 78 seats of 90) but picked up an additional 35 seats to secure government. Queensland Premier, Campbell Newman also lost his seat. It was one of the most astonishing election results in Australian political history and was considered to be an indication of what was likely to occur at the next federal election. After the Queensland election, there was a vote within the Liberal Party on 9 February 2015, calling for a leadership spill. The spill motion, was moved by Luke Simpkins and Don Randall, but was defeated by 61 votes to 39. Tony Abbott survived as Prime Minister.

Who are you?

25 February 2015

'**W**ho are you?'. A simple enough question and, in most cases, should elicit a straight forward response. When asked of a prime minister, however, it's a loaded question, existing on a plateau of minefields and acrobatic trickery that can establish the authority of a prime minister in the eyes of the electorate or, it can diminish them.

In a recent interview with the ABC *7.30*'s, Leigh Sales, 'who are you?' was a proposition put to Tony Abbott. Simple but elusive. Abbott failed to answer the question directly[1] but, in summary, alluded to what he is not: he's 'not Labor'.

This is a grand existential response, along the lines of a Derridian paradox: a nihilistic choice between the absence of presence, or the presence of absence. In this interview, Abbott is essentially saying: 'I am what I am not', or if one extends this to Cartesian thought, 'I think, therefore I am' becomes 'I do not think, therefore I am not'.

A simple situation but this lies at the heart of Tony Abbott's political problems and how it will be close to impossible to extricate himself from his predicament: his keen and pathological desire to define himself as 'not Labor', a hatred of

---

1   ABC Television, *7.30* 'Exclusive: Leigh Sales interviews PM Tony Abbott on 7.30' via YouTube. https://youtu.be/AUXxfTuX2oA

all things Labor, and a self-centred belief the entire community is behind his crusade to demonise and destroy Labor and any left-of-centre ideology.

A Liberal leadership spill was called for 9 February, the day that federal Parliament reconvened, and in the lead-up to the spill, Abbott repeated his claim: "we are not like Labor"… "we are not the Labor Party and we are not going to repeat the chaos and the instability of the Labor years", but not once did he state a positive or affirmative attribute: 'we are the Liberal Party'. Abbott survived this leadership spill vote in the absence of a challenger, only managing to gain 61 votes, against 39 votes and had, as he put it, "the near death experience". Apparently, 'good government' commenced the day after the spill, making us all wonder what the previous 521 days of the Liberal–National government had been all about.

So who is the Prime Minister? Surely after 18 months in office, and 21 years as a parliamentarian, there should be some skerrick of who the Prime Minister is, or what maketh the man. But with Abbott, there's a blank. What are his interests? Musical tastes? Books? Aside from clichéd biblical references, there's no indication of what his philosophical traditions are based on. Unlike his libertarian soul mates, who are quick to quote John Stuart Mill or John Locke, or predictably throw in Adam Smith's *Wealth of Nations* (as if these are the only philosophers they've ever read), there's no substance from Abbott, just a draconian anti-intellect that throws verbal grenades at passers by of a Labor or left-of-centre persuasion.

According to Liberal insider leaks to *The Australian*'s journalist John Lyon, Abbott sits for much of the day in his office in Parliament House[2] pondering national security, Islamic State and reading Churchill, while his Chief of Staff, Peta Credlin 'works the phones'. At least that's a hint of what Abbott might

---

2   John Lyons, *The Australian*, 'Tony Abbott in command, but is Peta Credlin in control?', 21 February 2015. http://www.theaustralian.com.au/news/features/tony-abbott-in-command-but-is-peta-credlin-in-control/story-e6frg6z6-1227233035933

be into, but do we really want our Prime Minister spending his days 'reading Churchill'? I'd suggest that he should start with Steven Covey's *The 7 Habits of Highly Effective People* to get some productivity underway, or at least a few serious contemporary management text books, because things are just not happening for him.

In recent days, Abbott's negative paradox has been extended to spiteful negativity, resulting in a vicious attack on the president of the Australian Human Rights Commission, Gillian Triggs. His behaviour indicates he is consumed by this hatred of the Labor Party, which has a natural extension to the hatred of human rights, and continues his hatred of high powered women that have achieved competence to a greater level than he has.

So while Tony Abbott can't say who he is, here's an outline of Gillian Triggs. Triggs is a prominent lawyer and a widely respected legal practitioner in the field of international civil rights, was a legal adviser in the development of the US *Civil Rights Act* and a barrister in Sydney, subsequently a Professor of Law at the University of Melbourne, and Dean of Law at the University of Sydney. She was appointed as president of the Australian Human Rights Commission in 2013.

In October 2014, Triggs presented to the government, *The Forgotten Children: National Inquiry into Children in Immigration Detention*,[3] which is at the heart of Abbott's current political outburst, where he claimed the report is 'a political stitch-up', conveniently ignoring the current stitch up of former Prime Ministers Julia Gillard and Kevin Rudd at the Royal Commissions into Trade Union Governance and Corruption[4] and the Home Insulation Scheme[5] (which, incidentally, are

3   Australian Human Rights Commission, 'The Forgotten Children: National Inquiry into Children in Immigration Detention, 2014. https://www.humanrights.gov.au/sites/default/files/document/publication/forgotten_children_2014.pdf

4   Royal Commission into Trade Union Governance and Corruption. http://www.tradeunionroyalcommission.gov.au/Pages/default.aspx

5   Royal Commission into the Home Insulation Program. http://www.homeinsulationroyalcommission.gov.au/Pages/default.html

costing the taxpayer over $100 million).

The Forgotten Children is a thorough report and is highly critical of both Labor and Liberal–National administrations on the issue of children in immigration detention. It accepts the issue of asylum seekers is politically vexed in Australia but provides a list of recommendations to the Australian Government which, of course, it is obliged to act upon. The report offers constructive advice to the government and a clear pathway towards solutions on a matter that is an obvious stain on the national psyche.

Judging by their overreactions and hostility, neither Tony Abbott nor his Attorney–General, George Brandis, appear to have read the report—certainly, the chairman of the Senate estimates, Liberal–National Senator Ian MacDonald hasn't, condemning the report—but then admitted he hadn't read it,[6] telling Sky News: "I don't waste my time reading documents I am going to take no notice of". Yes, these are all signs that we *are* witnessing a political stitch-up, but from the government, not from the Human Rights Commission.

And in another development, there have been reports that the government offered inducements to Triggs, in return for her resignation from the Human Rights Commission. It's a no-win situation for the government: attacking a respected practitioner who is standing up for the rights of children is not a good look. The attacks are a political beat-up that results in a net loss for the government, so why is Tony Abbott leading the way with an overly aggressive response to *The Forgotten Children* report?

As we've already ascertained, it's not possible for Abbott to position himself in a positive frame, he doesn't know who he is, and prefers to define himself by what he is not. Constructing a response to the Human Rights Commission report in a more prime ministerial manner, or creatively to achieve a positive outcome, is intellectually beyond his political skills set.

....

6   News.com.au, 'AG Brandis warns not everyone in the Government supports the HRC',
    24 February 2015. http://www.news.com.au/national/ag-brandis-warns-not-everyone-
    in-the-government-supports-the-hrc/story-fncynjr2-1227236992340

Another reason—Abbott is maniacally anti-Labor: Gillian Triggs was appointed by Labor in 2013, and the Human Rights Commission was created from a Labor initiative in 1986, which goes a long way to explaining his overreaction and accusations of bias: he is 'not Labor', after all. The removal of the Human Rights Commission is also number 82 on the Institute of Public Affairs' wonderful list of reactionary ideas[7] for government.

Since Abbott's self-styled 'near death experience', he has attempted to shore up his conservative parliamentary base. Many conservative members of Parliament in the Liberal–National Party despise the Human Rights Commission and attacking it is one way for Abbott to maintain and improve his leadership numbers within the party. This, along with his recent involvement with pseudo-nationalism, terrorism and anti-Islamic statements, proves once again that patriotism is the last refuge of a scoundrel, or at least, the last refuge for a prime minister with low approval ratings trying to get himself back into the game.[8]

All of this is quite pitiful. Abbott has no regard for anything except for himself. His leadership is paralysed by the continued leaks against him; more recently the resignation letter from honorary treasurer of the Liberal Party Phil Higginson[9] outlining the unsustainability of the leadership of Liberal Party director, Brian Loughnane, who is married to Abbott's Chief of Staff, Peta Credlin. Credlin and Loughnane were crucial to Abbott's path to the prime ministership but the skills required to be an effective Leader of the Opposition (albeit a negative one), are radically different to being an effective prime minister, a position that requires creative and lateral thinking to resolve

7   John Roskam, James Paterson & Chris Berg, Institute of Public Affairs, '25 more ideas for Tony Abbott'. https://ipa.org.au/publications/2110/25-more-ideas-for-tony-abbott

8   Simon Benson, *The Daily Telegraph*, 'Abbott is back in the game as Shorten's rating plunges', 23 February 2015. http://www.dailytelegraph.com.au/news/nsw/abbott-is-back-in-the-game-as-shortens-rating-plunges/story-fni0cx12-1227236244879

9   Philip Higginson, 22 February 2015. Honorary Federal Treasurer's Letter of Concern & Future Intention, https://www.documentcloud.org/documents/1673931-final-hft-letter-of-concern-and-intention-1-2.html

complex problems in the national interest. His first step after winning office should have been to create an effective team more suited to leading the nation, rather than the same team that mastered in small political squabbles, numbness and petty mindedness that suited Tony Abbott so well in Opposition. After all, he did see off two Labor Prime Ministers.

However, Tony Abbott as Leader of the Opposition, and Tony Abbott as Prime Minister, need to be different, but they are the same. The same team from Opposition is behind him, the same rhetoric and language that got him into office is still there, the same regressive reactionary negative mode of leadership is still there, and it has left him ill-equipped to handle the office of Prime Minister.

That's why we see Abbott targeting his fury at the Human Rights Commissioner and her report, a report which he could have chosen to make inconsequential by sweeping it under the carpet, but chose instead to nail his negativity on its cover. He knows nothing else. And it's the reason why he targets Islam and Islamic leaders: an easy target, considering Muslims constitute only 1 per cent of the national population. It's also the same method John Howard used to target the Indigenous community during the Wik land title negotiations in 1998, claiming private backyards were at risk of land title claims.

So, Tony Abbott might not know who he is, but we certainly do. He's the desperate leader, scraping for survival, searching for any rabbit hole and sewer pipe to prop up his disastrous leadership. He's the anti-intellect who looks for easy targets, because he knows they're weakened in their abilities to respond. He's the one who is the tribal leader of the Liberal Party and thinks that problems from his predecessors are "a classic example of what goes wrong when in a fit of absent-mindedness, people elect Labor governments".[10]

---

10   Joanna Heath & Adam Rollason, *Australian Financial Review*, 'Tony Abbott speaks at National Press Club', 2 February 2015. http://www.afr.com/p/national/tony_abbott_speaks_at_national_press_iEp2bjb5x0IISSWmVaO1XJ

Political history in Australia has shown that prime ministers never recover from leadership challenges. They might hang in for a few more months (or, in Malcolm Fraser's case after being challenged by Andrew Peacock in 1981, almost 18 months) but they inevitably go. Abbott has lost credibility within his party, and the Australian electorate and, worst of all for him, has become the source of ongoing ridicule.[11] Abbott's intense hatred of Labor will eventually destroy him. There'll be leadership speculation every time Parliament sits in Canberra or whenever the next gaff or 'captain's call' appears on the horizon. It's just a matter of time.

*

---

11 Scott Limbrick, *Junkee*, 'Tony Abbott's Biggest Problem Isn't Trust; It's Ridicule', 18 February 2015. http://junkee.com/tony-abbotts-biggest-problem-isnt-trust-its-ridicule/51300

Thank goodness Anzac Day is over

26 April 2015

Anzac Day is over for another year, and thank goodness for that. Being the 100th year since the landing at Gallipoli in 1915, there was always a high possibility that this year's commemorations were going to be extreme in the media, at Gallipoli, in the suburbs and, of course, a grand opportunity for political leaders of all persuasions to cover themselves with the Anzac aura, and take us down the path of a perverse form of war-porn.

The Gallipoli landing, and the deaths of around 400 Australian soldiers on 25 April 1915 (officially 860 between 25–30 April, and 8,704 during the full eight-month campaign at Gallipoli), is truly a national tragedy and a significant historical event in Australian history. But, as was the case in 1914 when Prime Minister Andrew Fisher, and then Prime Minister Billy Hughes, made the calls that Australia needed to make the 'blood sacrifice' by offering its young soldiers to the British Empire, militarism in Australia and Anzac Day has been hi-jacked by the political class—from Fisher, Hughes, and Robert Menzies, to Bob Hawke, John Howard and now Tony Abbott—for self-aggrandisement and political benefit. And the Australian public has, largely, been taken for the ride.

Anzac Day (and the legend of the Anzacs) has taken on a quasi-religious mysteriousness, where factually incorrect events from military history have taken on their own level of verity, the sexualisation of Anzac Day has been deemed to be offensive, and the commercialisation of any form of Anzac iconography has led to public outrage and abuse.

Zoo Magazine is not my preference of leisure reading, but their 'special commemorative issue' cover for Anzac Day featured a female model in a bikini holding a poppy was called 'gross, disgusting and idiotic'[1] on social media. So the untold stories of rape and pillage by Australia soldiers during military campaigns, as well as having the worst reputation for treatment of prisoners of war during World War I, is a fine and noble pursuit, but a semi-soft-porn lampooning threatens our sensibilities, horrifies us and leads to public censorship? Perhaps the high levels of venereal disease of soldiers returning from the battlefield might be a source for some of our concern as well?

The Woolworths supermarket chain was targeted for its 'Fresh in our memories' campaign, which placed those words over images of former soldiers. One user on Twitter asked: 'Is Anzac Day really a commercial opportunity?' Well, yes, of course it is. Haven't you seen VB's 'Raise A Glass' campaign, running each year since 2009? Yes, that's the one our current Governor–General, Peter Cosgrove, appeared in.

The people complaining about the commercialisation of Anzac Day are probably the same ones that munch on a hot-cross bun months before Easter, stock up on chocolate eggs in readiness for the egg hunt on Easter Sunday, and join into the mad rush to purchase presents for Christmas and Christkindl.

Anzac beer mugs, t-shirts, slouch hats, football jerseys, rings—all available for many months at Target, KMart and… Woolworths. The online audience almost caused an internet meltdown with its outrage about the Woolworths 'Fresh in our

---

1   Anthony Colangelo, *New Daily*, 'Zoo Magazine slammed for 'disgusting' Anzac cover', 24 April 2015. http://thenewdaily.com.au/news/2015/04/24/zoo-magazine-anzac-edition

memories' campaign. Again, these are the same people that would probably readily buy specially manufactured Anzac Day sausages—no different to sausages made on any other day—t-shirts and other gaudy Anzac Day paraphernalia... but it's the use of the word 'fresh' that causes the greatest offense.

The SBS sports journalist, Scott McIntyre, was sacked for Twitter messages he posted on 25 April. In summary, they were:

@mcintinhos 5:39 PM – 25 Apr 2015 | *The cultification of an imperialist invasion of a foreign nation that Australia had no quarrel with is against all ideals of modern society.*

Yes, this is actually true. In 1914, Australia had no issue with the Ottoman Empire, and it was primarily a British imperialist adventure. Whether or not one feels that war has been 'cultified' (and I believe it has been), war-mongering is against the principles of a modern society.

@mcintinhos 5:39 PM – 25 Apr 2015 | *Wonder if the poorly-read, largely white, nationalist drinkers and gamblers pause today to consider the horror that all mankind suffered.*

I'm not one to do surveys, but I'd say it's probably true. In Kate Aubusson's ABC documentary, *Lest We Forget What?*,[2] the first 10 minutes documents young Australians preparing for the dawn service at Anzac Cove and, judging by that, I'd say yes: poorly-read, largely white, nationalist drinkers. No idea at all. While I don't think it's a great documentary, it's excellent in its appraisal of the critical question: what are we exactly commemorating on Anzac Day? Certainly not the Aboriginal people that served at Gallipoli, or the Australian–Chinese.

2   Rainer the Cabbie, *The Big Smoke Australia*, 'What is the ANZAC legend?', 22 April 2015.
    http://thebigsmoke.com.au/2015/04/22/anzac-legend

@mcintinhos 5:40 PM – 25 Apr 2015 | *Remembering the summary execution, widespread rape and theft committed by these 'brave' Anzacs in Egypt, Palestine and Japan.*

Yes, sad to say, this is correct but it's an inconvenient truth. The Surafend massacre was committed by Anzac soldiers in 1918—as were the executions of prisoners in German New Guinea[3] in 1914. A list of atrocities committed by Australian soldiers[4] can be found online, and more extensive details can be found in A.K. Madougall's excellent book, *Australians at War: A pictorial history*.

Now, this is not to say that these acts were exceptional: atrocities of all kinds happen during war and nationality is no barrier to the worst kinds of human depravity being committed on the battlefield—that's the disgusting nature of war, whether you agree with war or not. Essentially, McIntyre was accused of insulting our perceptions of Anzac soldiers being pure and infallible when, in reality, they were committing all sorts of war crimes that were up there with the infamous rapes of Nanking in 1937/38.

@mcintinhos 5:40 PM – 25 Apr 2015 | *Not forgetting that the largest single-day terrorist attacks in history were committed by this nation & their allies in Hiroshima & Nagasaki*

Well, this is such a large part of common understandings of the history of World War II that it's difficult to see why anyone would disagree with it... unless they didn't know about it. Around 130,000 people died in those two cities in one day. United States Major General Curtis LeMay ordered the bombing of these two cities, even though Japan was on the verge of surrender.

....

3   ABC Radio National, *RN Breakfast*, 'Claims Australians executed prisoners in WWI engagement', 11 September 2014. http://www.abc.net.au/radionational/programs/breakfast/claims-of-australian-war-crimes-in-first-wwi-engagement/5734180

4   Tom Orsag, *Solidarity*, 'Australian atrocities at war', 19 September 2008. http://www.solidarity.net.au/reviews/australian-atrocities-at-war

And this was preceded by the deaths of 100,000 people during the Tokyo firebombings. Everyone knows about this... *don't* they?

> @mcintinhos 5:41 PM – 25 Apr 2015 | *Innocent children, on the way to school, murdered. Their shadows seared into the concrete of Hiroshima.*

Yes, unfortunately, this was the side-effect of people being attacked by atomic bombs in Hiroshima. People were vapourised by these bombings, and left shadows in the concrete. I'd also say that Japanese children would not have had any quarrel with the Allied forces, were on their way to school and, by definition of what constitutes war criminality (even at that stage, by the League of Nations) were murdered. But, as war history is written by the victors, this was never deemed to be a war crime, and show trials were held for German, Italian and Japanese military commanders, but not for American, British or Australian commanders.

So, Scott McIntyre's comments from his Twitter account are totally correct, even if some of his comments do add a bit of opinionated spice. His comments have been labelled 'despicable', 'insensitive', 'immature', 'offensive', 'deserve to be condemned' and 'gutless'.

Even the libertarian Human Rights Commissioner, Tim Wilson, who has defended everyone's right to say the most offensive statements to anyone, believes in this case, McIntyre's freedom of speech should be curtailed. "We're talking about political interpretations of history and that is open for debate," Wilson said. "And he will be judged very harshly." *Naughty boy!*

And then, in the lead up to Anzac Day, we had the spectacle of the Minister for Foreign Affairs, Julie Bishop, visiting the offices of Charlie Hebdo, congratulating them and defending their right to freedom of speech and expression. Now, I don't believe any journalist or any cartoonist should be murdered for expressing their views and it would be very helpful if Islamic fundamentalists developed a sense of humour. But perhaps if an Arabic cartoonist depicted an Anzac digger being anally raped by the devil, we might start to understand why Islamists were so offended by Charlie Hebdo's extreme and vile anti-Islamic cartoons.

So, there are definitely double standards here, but who's really being 'gutless' here? McIntyre for telling us the inconvenient truth? All of those facile political leaders for jumping on the bandwagon with their feigned condemnations? Tim Wilson and his selective ideas of what constitutes 'freedom of speech'? Or Major General Curtis LeMay in 1945 for ordering the release of an atomic bomb from the comfort of the B-29 *Enola Gay*, flying silently 10,000 metres above Hiroshima, and killing 130,000 innocent Japanese civilians?

I think we've lost our perspective and put aside good sense if we're prepared to attack and vilify a SBS sports journalist for prickling our national conscience on a day that has been confected and manufactured and littered with historical falsehoods, sport, alcohol, commercialism and jingoism.

The vainglorious, macho, chauvinist and racist nature of Anzac Day commemorations will be with us for a long time and, perhaps never be weeded out. Don't get me wrong: the landing at Gallipoli in 1915 is a very significant event for Australia, and the real history of Australia at war is as fascinating and exciting as any other country's. But the event itself has been subsumed by a legend of unreality, a version that is both fairy floss and pornographic at the same time. Like most of the historical writing of Australian history, where the poor treatment of Aboriginal people and anything deemed to deflect from the idea of the 'perfect' Australia has been excluded, we've been fed schlock and happily accept it for the sake of creating an idyllic national identity.

We don't know really what we're commemorating and Anzac Day has become our most revered and pseudo-religious day. It's almost like subservient Catholics continuing their church service each Sunday, without fully understanding Catholicism, or to ever question the existence of God.

Anzac Day now means that journalists are sacked if they dare to utter known historical facts, or bring up matters of inconvenience, as if there is a new right-wing political correctness that demands unquestioning venal behaviour, even if the facade of historical incorrectness is propped up by tacky commercialism and opportunists who want to cash in on Anzac-ery, without having the faintest idea of what it all means. I even had two women in green and gold face paint say 'Happy Anzac Day' to me on the streets of Burwood—I don't think it's meant to be a 'happy' day. In classic middle-class NIMBY style, we genuflect at the altar of militarism, happy to celebrate far-away wars, a form of rose-coloured nostalgia that is great fun, as long it doesn't affect housing prices in our major cities and the shops still open after the Anzac Day services are over. There's something wrong with all of this.

Richard Clutterbuck was an academic and, perhaps, the preeminent researcher in the study of political violence. The opening words of his 1993 book *International Crisis and Conflict* are: 'War is mass lunacy'. Rather than military campaigns being won or lost, or becoming part of a national vernacular (such as the Anzac Day phenomenon in Australia), war must be seen as a failure of the political system and, especially of the politicians that wage war. It's at the time of Anzac Day that we tend to forget this critical issue, and it's this factor that need to change.

*

Abbott's Royal Commission losing credibility by the day

1 September 2015

Just when we thought the ridicule floating around the Royal Commission into Trade Union Governance and Corruption might have ended, it was surely added to today. The Commissioner, former Justice of the High Court of Australia, Dyson Heydon, adjudicated that despite being a guest speaker at the annual Garfield Barwick Address (a Liberal Party-initiated event hosted from 2010 onwards), he will continue with his commission until its completion, ruling that "it is not the case that a fair-minded lay observer might apprehend that I might not bring an impartial mind" to the inquiry. This severely compromises his position as an independent commissioner.

However, if Dyson Heydon really understood how a fair-minded person might think, he would understand this imaginary person would believe otherwise, considering he was appointed to the High Court in 2003 by the Howard government; both of his parents were staff to former Liberal Party minister, Ron Casey, and Heydon was on the panel that approved the Rhodes Scholarship for Tony Abbott in 1980. His father was also the private secretary to Robert Menzies. And although self-ruling in this situation is an acceptable legal protocol, the fair-minded person might conclude that it's totally outrageous that Heydon can decide by himself whether he can continue with his commission, especially at the handsome fee of $3,000 per day.

Aside from his innate conservatism, it would be hard to find someone on the political spectrum more diametrically opposite to the Labor Party and the union movement. Heydon was also legal adviser to Australians for a Constitutional Monarchy, and worked with Tony Abbott in the campaign against the republic referendum in 1999. In 2013, at the right-wing think-tank Centre for Independent Studies, he claimed that the 'Rudd government was non-substansive' and criticised the Gillard government about various bills in Parliament, and its spending patterns. He's a Liberal man, through and through.

Due to speak at the annual Garfield Barwick address, an event organised by the Liberal Party, and promoted as a fundraiser for the Liberal Party, Heydon claims that he wasn't aware that it was a fundraiser and should not lead to the average ordinary person thinking that he might be, in any way, biased.

His main rebuttal to the claim that he received emails about his speaking appointment at the Garfield Barwick Address, which clearly indicated that it was a Liberal Party fundraiser (and he should have aware of this), was that he does not own or use a computer and he is incapable of sending or receiving emails: "the consequence is that I read emails only after they have been printed out for me" (his private secretary prints out his emails for him). We can accept that someone in their 70s is probably not going to be the most technologically literate person around but, in 2015, many older Australians have acquired the skills to read and create emails.

In political speak that would do his masters proud, Dyson added that: "Further, the fair-minded observer would recognise that I was busily engaged in Commission work. The contention that, having regard to those matters, the fair-minded observer would necessarily infer that I read the invitation is fanciful."

Dismissive, arrogant, loose with the facts, dismissing that a supposedly 'fair-minded observer' would have any reason to question his credibility, or his 'unbiased mind'.

This, of course, is all quite foolish, and more consistent with a political rebuttal, rather than a legal one. Despite the denials of Tony Abbott and Attorney–General George Brandis, this Royal Commission has entirely been set up as a political exercise to discredit the Labor Party. The timetable has been developed to enable the release of a report around the time of the next election. Heydon attempted to humiliate former Prime Minister Julia Gillard by admonishing her for not having a clear memory of minor events from over 20 years ago, harassed current Labor Leader of the Opposition, Bill Shorten, about his 'credibility as a witness' and presided over the Royal Commission as though he was an extension of Abbott's political Praetorian Guard.

The Royal Commission has been seriously tarnished, whether Dyson Heydon is to stay, or whether he is to go. But, the main spotlight has been placed onto Tony Abbott. Whether the Royal Commission was to find anything worthwhile about corruption within the trade union movement is immaterial— there are many other avenues to seek where corruption lies, and establishing a Royal Commission is probably the least effective. But, as a blunt instrument to apply a blowtorch against your political opponents—rolling media coverage, unsavoury characters hauled in front of the Commission, all of your political enemies lined up like a Nuremberg-style show trial— there's nothing better... with one caveat. That it needs to be run properly and above politics, and Abbott's management of the Commission has been far from this.

Firstly, if Abbott was genuine about the Royal Commission, Heydon's commission should have been terminated immediately, and a new commissioner installed—he's been severely compromise, as has the reputation of this Royal Commission. By being loyal to Heydon, Abbott has been caught up in another scandal of his own making. Perhaps he had memories of the Royal Commission on the Activities of the

Federated Ship Painters and Dockers Union in the 1980s, which started off as a witch-hunt into the affairs of corrupt unions, but the commissioner, Frank Costigan, veered into bottom-of-the-harbour schemes and netted other corrupt behaviours of corporate Australia (and Liberal Party donors).

By going for overkill, Abbott has exposed his main political weaknesses—impatience, a total inflexibility to new strategies, and very few tools at his disposal to negate any poor political news or the political events that don't (usually) go to plan, or to adequately prosecute a case for the re-election of his government.

A case in point is the recent Operation Fortitude, where Australian Border Force staff were due to be positioned in the Melbourne central business district and, according to their press release (yes, a press release!) will be 'speaking with any individual we cross paths with', apparently looking for people overstaying their visa conditions. Perhaps it was the macho-bravado, but many people viewed it initially as a prank—I certainly did. The entire operation descended into farce and fiasco, and within hours, a humiliating cancellation and official backdown, a series of blame-games, and then the admission that the Minister responsible for Australian Border Force, Peter Dutton, hadn't even read the press release about Operation Fortitude before it went out. Aside from this, why the Australian Border Force would telegraph its intentions so clearly to the public was never explained.

(For history buffs, the original Operation Fortitude during Word War II was a deception to trick the Germans into diverting their armies away from Normandy. It's hard to imagine what the deception might have been in Melbourne but it's probably best to stick with stuff-up, rather than conspiracy. After all, there is no war currently in Melbourne).

And these same people in government, the ones that can't even organise a sting to catch taxi-drivers overstaying their visas in downtown Melbourne, now want to send fighter planes for airstrikes over Syria.[1] The following day, Abbott kept to the script: it was 'a poorly worded press release' responsible for the chaos. He managed to conflate the issue with 'stopping the boats', repealing the carbon tax, small business incentives and, like the drowning man clutching at the straw, threw in 'infrastructure' for good measure.

And here lies the problem for Tony Abbott and the Liberal Party: lack of an agenda. At every opportunity, two key points, border security (boats) and carbon tax, are wrapped around the issue of the day and, as if to realise that ain't enough, more disparate and abstract ideas are added to the spiel. Almost two years into his prime ministership, all Tony Abbott can offer is a rerun of the issues from the 2013 election, with two new catchphrases tacked on: small business and infrastructure.

Desperation is the first element the electorate sniffs from a poorly-performing prime minister, and Abbott has this written all over him. Just repeating the mantra 'better than Labor', and revisiting old agendas from past elections just won't wash with the electorate. The reported request for 'weekly security announcements'[2] from the Australian Federal Policy between now and the next election shows that the government is bereft of ideas, and wasted all of that time in Opposition during 2007–2013 working out how to get back into government, rather than working what they would do once they got there.

If only they'd completed their homework during those long years in Opposition, the Liberal Party would not be in their current predicament—they've been behind in the polls for the past 18 months, and facing a loss of 36 seats at the next election. Preselecting military people into by-elections (such as former

1   Mark Kenny & David Wroe, *Sydney Morning Herald*, 'Tony Abbott pushed for US request to join Syria air strikes', 26 August 2015. http://www.smh.com.au/federal-politics/political-news/tony-abbott-pushed-for-us-request-to-join-syrian-air-strikes-20150825-gj7kfh.html

2   Laura Tingle, *Australian Financial Review*, 'Tony Abbott: determined to lead the Whitlam government of our time?', 13 August 2015. http://www.afr.com/opinion/columnists/laura-tingle/tony-abbott-determined-to-lead-the-whitlam-government-of-our-time-20150813-giy574

Australian Army officer Andrew Hastie in the WA seat of Canning), wanting engagement in faraway wars in unknown places, creating havoc with Border Force, repeating 'death cult' endlessly, and promoting *faux* militarisation of politics can always work if a government is seen as competent, and has an underlying bed of achievement.

But this government hasn't got that. Tony Abbott can keep trying to put border security and the military at the forefront of his government and in the mind of the electorate. Try as he might, it's just not going to work. Not even by donning military fatigues and leading the SAS to the frontline in the desert. The electorate is cynical and can see that beyond this thin veneer, there is nothing else. Absolutely nothing.

*

Malcolm Turnbull challenged Tony Abbott on 14 September 2015 and won the Liberal Party leadership ballot by 54 votes to 44 on the following day. Tony Abbott's tenure as Prime Minister lasted three days short of two years. During his final media conference as Prime Minister, Abbott said "my pledge today is to make this change as easy as I can. There will be no wrecking, no undermining, and no sniping. I've never leaked or backgrounded against anyone. And I certainly won't start now."

Turnbull is not the man the media wants us to believe

5 December 2015

One of my greatest bugbears is getting off trains during peak period. As you're trying to get off the train when it arrives at your station, there's always a crush of passengers at the platform pushing to get on. *If only they could wait until passengers got off the train*, I always think, *there'd be more room for them and easier for them to get on.* It would be more orderly and, instead of trying to defy the laws of physics, they'd be saving time. But, no, they're impatient and, I'd even go so far to suggest that they lack one critical aspect: judgement.

In the haste to *get onto that train*, they'll push and barge, desperate to get that last surviving seat or, at least *get onto that train*, lest it disappears into the ether and they're left behind, contemplating whether the next train will arrive in three or eight minutes. But, trains being trains, will wait until this exchange is complete: the train waits until all people that want to get off, are off, and all those people wanting to get on, are on. Whether it's an orderly process, or chaotic, the train waits.

The behaviour of the media has reminded me of this chaos, ever since Malcolm Turnbull ousted Tony Abbott to become Australia's 29th Prime Minister on 15 September. He's number 29, but he may as well be number one, so enamoured is the media with him.

The media has seamlessly moved from the being the self-appointed sycophants when Tony Abbott was Prime Minister, to the self-appointed new Praetorian Guard of Malcolm Turnbull: guileless, defensive, fashionable, and prepared to fend away any criticism of the leader. This new Praetorian Guard is everywhere to be seen: we see it at the ABC, we see it at Fairfax media and, from an institution that should know better, *The Guardian*.

The reporting of Turnbull's recent overseas 'whirlwind tour' by *The Guardian*'s Katharine Murphy is gushing journalism at its worst. Not only is the journalist embedded with the Prime Minister's entourage, but embeds herself into the story.[1] Less gushing, but who should also know better is Lenore Taylor, also at *The Guardian*. For Taylor, 'intelligence' again seems to be the key.[2]

Also in *The Guardian*'s fantasy land is Osman Faruqi, who seems to feel that charm is far more preferable than policies of substance, and asking 'why would Australians trust a former union boss [Bill Shorten] who smells like shady deals rather than an actual entrepreneur when it comes to startups and innovation policy?'.[3] That's a good one—where is this evidence of being 'an actual entrepreneur'? Turnbull had the good fortune to invest in OzEmail and sell at the right time. He's not an entrepreneur like, say Dick Smith, Bill Gates or Steve Jobs. 'Innovation policy'? Excuse me? Again, where is this evidence of 'innovation policy'. That's right, it doesn't exist, unless you consider a few door-stop interviews discussing start-ups to be evidence of 'policy'.

1   Katharine Murphy, *The Guardian*, 'Presidents, planes – and Paris. Inside the whirlwind of Malcolm Turnbull's first world tour', 20 November 2015. http://www.theguardian.com/australia-news/2015/nov/20/presidents-planes-and-paris-inside-the-whirlwind-of-malcolm-turnbulls-first-world-tour

2   Lenore Taylor, *The Guardian*, 'Labor's leadership dilemma as Turnbull's star burns bright', 30 November 2015. http://www.theguardian.com/australia-news/2015/oct/30/leadership-a-study-of-contrasts

3   Osman Faruqi, *The Guardian*, 'Turnbull's unstoppable charm can't be beaten – only bypassed', 29 October 2015. http://www.theguardian.com/commentisfree/2015/oct/29/turnbulls-unstoppable-charm-cant-be-beaten-only-bypassed

Another sucked into Turnbull's charm offensive is Marius Benson at the ABC—his story titled 'Voting for Mr T'[4] is filled with repetitive gloating about the character of the new Prime Minister: "Turnbull just glided seamlessly into the post and set about gently adjusting the pulleys and levers of power to nudge the ship of state into new directions. Anything but daunted".

This really is terrible journalism and signs off with: "he [Turnbull] looks good for two or three election wins from here". Really? Why two or three? Why not four? Or one? Or seven? Critical analysis or just a hunch?

Also in the vortex and ushering in 'a new era'[5] is the ABC's Barry Cassidy—although his more recent articles have shown more sensibility—and the even more seasoned journalists such as Paul Bongiorno have joined the caravan, defending another journalist in a Twitter spat (who was chastised for being too fawning) by replying: "So to recognise intelligent leadership is fawning! Utterly pathetic".

There are many more that could be mentioned here (ABC's *7.30* is a serial offender—no wonder former ABC presenter Kerry O'Brien decided to leave this sorry saga of a broadcaster behind) but my favourite for the most obsequious piece of journalism for the year (and possibly the decade) goes to (among very tough competition) Elizabeth Farrelly's piece in the *Sydney Morning Herald*,[6] for claiming that Malcolm Turnbull will "be our longest-serving PM since Robert Menzies" and how "it is such a relief to have a leader who uses intelligence to connect with the rest of us". Mmm. No mention of any of Turnbull's many

....

4   Marius Benson, ABC News, 'Turnbull settles into his most acclaimed role yet', 20 November 2015. http://www.abc.net.au/news/2015-11-20/benson-turnbull-settles-into-his-most-acclaimed-role-yet/6957220

5   Barry Cassidy, ABC News, 'Welcome to the new, positive era of Australian politics. No really', 20 November 2015. http://www.abc.net.au/news/2015-11-20/cassidy-welcome-to-the-new,-positive-era-of-australian-politics/6956820

6   Elizabeth Farrelly, *Sydney Morning Herald*, 'Why Malcolm Turnbull will be our longest-serving PM since Robert Menzies', 25 November 2015. http://www.smh.com.au/comment/why-malcolm-turnbull-will-be-our-longestserving-pm-since-robert-menzies-20151125-gl7dy2.html

failures, which we'll get to shortly. *Be patient! Show some judgement!*

I've only selected a few samples here, but you get the picture—it's hard to avoid reading in print or on screen, or seeing on our televisions, or listening through radios—anything but blind gushing gonzo journalistic praise of Malcolm Turnbull, and it's largely devoid of analytic perspective, or context of real political issues.

This sentiment is akin to groupies following a pop star, like courtiers waiting on every word, not quite like bumbling jesters from an early episode of *Black Adder*, but very close:

Increasing the GST by 50 per cent to 15 per cent GST? Don't worry about that, we have an intelligent Prime Minister!...

...No fines for companies that fail to fulfill their superannuation obligations? Oh, come on, we now have a beautiful looking Prime Minister: he's so good looking!...

...Inappropriate investments in the Cayman Islands? You disgust me, how dare you question the Prime Minister's grand intentions!...

...Direct Action is still in place? Who cares, look at those loins... I want to bite them!

It's a pity Gerard Henderson never heeds his own advice, but he recently did complain on ABC's *Insiders* that he'd 'never seen so much fawning about a new Prime Minister', not since Gough Whitlam... 'journalists are not meant to be barrackers'. Too right, Gerard and it's hard to disagree on this occasion.

And all this sycophancy takes politics to a dangerous place, where personalities become more important for journalists to report on, rather than assessing, dissecting and analysing the real policies that affect real people. In other words, where the real politics exists. It could be argued that political reporting has always been based on the personalities that make up and play the game, but this has reached a new low.

So, why does this new level of fawning exist, and why this grand push to let the public know how 'intelligent' Malcolm

Turnbull supposedly is? Shouldn't we expect all of our prime ministers to be 'intelligent'? I can't recall much discussion in the media about Julia Gillard's intelligence (oh, that's right: better to talk about what she's wearing, or about yet another moronic teenager throwing a Vegemite sandwich at her during a school visit).

Of course, it's the old practice of political journalism: write the good stuff, journalist gets the access, and continues to get the leads, the stories—which keeps them in their jobs. That's the way it has always been but more and more, the public interest has taken the back seat and, like a tragic opera, the interplay between personalities and infotainment has become paramount. But it's much much more than that.

In her recent Quarterly Essay, *Political Amnesia: How we forgot to govern*, Fairfax journalist Laura Tingle bemoans the loss of corporate memory within the public service when governments change and implement their respective versions of the 'night of the long knives', and the related issue of the cultural and political amnesia of mainstream journalists.

I'd also add that political journalists have become oblivious to their own inanity and partisanship, almost as though they've watched too many episodes of the US television series, *The West Wing*, and writing about political pantomime in the style of television scriptwriter Aaron Sorkin is a fiction far better to believe that what's really happening on the ground.

So, what should the media be reporting? Instead of posting what they *think* Turnbull should be or could be, based on figments of the imagination (or attempting to conflate the fiction of *The West Wing*'s Jed Bartlet with the fiction of Malcolm Turnbull), what about writing about what he *actually is* ?

Next time a journalist claims Malcolm Turnbull is 'intelligent', remind them of his track record, which shows anything but intelligence and, most importantly, a severe lack of judgement.

Let's start in 2008.

Malcolm Turnbull was a disaster as Leader of the Opposition during 2008–2009. There's no denying this. To get to the position, he hounded the previously elected leader of the Liberal Party, Brendan Nelson, on a regular basis, calling on him to 'muscle up' and 'toughen up', or resign.

When Nelson finally resigned and Turnbull became leader, Turnbull simply wasn't up to the job. He overcooked his case. He was impatient. He lacked judgement. He had no reading of the character of Godwin Grech, the public servant at the centre of the OzCar affair who provided fabricated emails alleging Labor Party corruption, and was guided through this debacle by Senator Eric Abetz, a gormless conservative political partisan who brings little talent or skill to Parliament. To believe that he could bring down the Rudd government based on flimsy evidence (and, as it turned out, false evidence) from an ill and sad lightweight Treasury official says a lot about Turnbull's political judgement.

When he was ousted by the Liberal Party in late 2009, he was only preferred by 14 per cent of the electorate to be Prime Minister, and had the Liberal–National Party battling at 43 per cent of the two party preferred vote (Newspoll 27–29 November, 2009).

I can see that there wasn't much intelligence or judgement then.

The return of Blinky Bill

The Australian republic referendum in 1999, complete with recalling Blinky Bill (yes, *Blinky Bill!*) as the campaign's mascot (why a political campaign needs a mascot was never fully explained, but Turnbull did state that Blinky Bill is 'quintessentially Australian'), was another political disaster and resulted in a sound defeat—54.87 per cent of the electorate voted 'No', and the vote was not carried in any state (ACT voted 63 per cent in favour of becoming a republic, but being a territory, it doesn't register).

Turnbull was president of the Australian Republican Movement and spearheaded the campaign. This was more evidence of Turnbull's poor political skills—an issue that had clear support within the community at the time, but one which Turnbull allowed to be hijacked by the Direct Election camp, stubbornly refusing to consider any possibility of a direct election of a republican president, even though 80 per cent of people in polls said they would only support a republic if they could vote directly for the president.

Subsequently, Turnbull blamed then Prime Minister Howard for the defeat and said: "history will remember him [Howard] for one thing. He was the Prime Minister who broke this nation's heart". No, it wasn't Howard, it was Turnbull's intransigence, stubbornness and lack of ability to understand what was required to bring about the republic in Australia. If 80 per cent of electors preferred to directly vote for the president, rather that having the president appointed by two-thirds majority of the Parliament, then Turnbull should have worked towards this model, and codified the powers of the president to achieve this. Mathematical and political logic suggests that in this case, give the people what they want. But he didn't.

Not much intelligence or judgement here either and this defeat in 1999 pushed the republican cause back by 20–30 years.

Old copper the way of Turnbull's internet future

Not enough people in the electorate understand the difference between fibre-to-the-node (FTTN) and fibre-to-the-premises (FTTP), and the difference between the plans presented by Labor and the Coalition at the 2013 federal election. If they did, Malcolm Turnbull would have been hounded out of office by now. To be sure, the National Broadband Network was a political mess that was passed onto Turnbull. I say a 'political mess', because Labor in office never effectively prosecuted the case for the importance of the NBN (understandable, since they were more intent on removing Kevin Rudd and consigning themselves to the Opposition benches again, than concentrating fully on promoting their policies). Technically though, and as a technological and social service, it was the correct path and correct project to build and, when completed, would put Australia on the same trajectory as South Korea, currently the country with the fastest broadband speeds in the world. It would replace copper wiring with fibre, however, at a huge cost—$90 billion in 2013 terms.

Turnbull's management of the NBN as Minister for Communications was to introduce a hybrid of existing copper wiring, replacing some old copper wiring, and introducing fibre-to-the-node. It's likely the entire network of copper wiring will have to be replaced at some point in the near future, meaning a government of the future will have to embark on this project again.

There is a perception of Malcolm Turnbull being a champion of the corporate world and private sector entrepreneurship, but the management of the NBN project under his watch has been another disaster. Fortunately for Turnbull, the technical literacy of the electorate is not high, and it's hard to measure the political cost of something (such as super-fast broadband) that people don't have as yet, and are unaware of what the technological benefits could be in the future.

During the 2013 election campaign, Tony Abbott introduced Malcolm Turnbull as 'the man who virtually invented the internet in Australia'[7] (yes, he actually said that, quite a few times).

Of course, Turnbull did no such thing—there's a massive difference between being an investor (which is what Turnbull was with OzEmail) and having a firm understanding of technology. Just because Turnbull is adept at managing his HTC phone, Twitter and Facebook accounts, and knows which buttons he needs to press on his iPad (along with millions of

---

7   Breaking Politics, 'Tony Abbott: Malcolm Turnbull 'virtually invented the internet in this country' via YouTube. https://youtu.be/18owzYfvIcE

other Australians), it doesn't mean that he knows anything more about the internet than you or I.

Someone who 'virtually invented the internet in Australia' ended his tenure as Minister for Communications as the man who virtually destroyed the internet in Australia.

No sign of intelligence or judgement here either.

Nothing stands in the way of Malcolm

Intelligent? How about being an outright bastard, opportunist and prepared to knock out anything and anyone standing in his way, including an internationally respected Palestinian politician?

It would be interesting to hear Peter King's perspective on Malcolm Turnbull. In 2003, King was the sitting Liberal member in the seat of Wentworth, and after being told by Turnbull to "fuck off and get out of my way"[8] (strangely similar words to the ones that Turnbull kindly mentioned to Brendan Nelson in 2008—you can see that there's a pattern forming here), suffered a political assassination at the hands of Turnbull and lost his preselection for the 2004 election—despite an unwritten protocol that sitting members of the Liberal Party should not be challenged in preselections.

The Turnbulls (yes, Turnbull's wife Lucy, then Lord Mayor of Sydney, joined in the political attack as well)[9] were out of control, doing whatever they could to win the seat of Wentworth, even going to the great effort of attacking and denigrating the recipient of that year's Sydney Peace Prize, Palestinian academic, international human rights activist, and politician, Dr Hanan Ashrawi, to receive preselection favour from the large Jewish enclave that reside in the seat of Wentworth.

Ambition? Yes. Dignity and judgment? No evidence here.

8   Brett Evans, *Inside Story*, 'The Battle For Wentworth', 19 September 2015. http://insidestory.org.au/the-battle-for-wentworth

9   Alan Ramsey, *Sydney Morning Herald*, 'Here's Lucy, caving in, taking flight', 25 October 2003. http://www.smh.com.au/articles/2003/10/24/1066974313719.html

Perhaps if journalists could recover their memories, this sordid event could be replayed whenever Turnbull ever brings out the 'international statesman' card, or offers commentary on the Israel–Palestinian question.

*

Now, for all of this critique, Malcolm Turnbull *could* turn out to be a great Prime Minister. And, there's always a possibility that he *could* become the longest-serving Prime Minister in Australia's history, in the same way that anyone in Australia could. Admittedly, he would have a much better chance than you or I, but it's still very unlikely. Elizabeth Farrelly decreed that Turnbull would become the longest-serving Prime Minister since Robert Menzies (yes, I'll have what she's having).

For this to occur, he'd have to remain Prime Minister until early 2027 (when he'd surpass John Howard's 11 years and 267 days) and win the next four elections—he'd be pushing the age of 73, also making him the oldest serving Prime Minister in our history. In another fit of blind mindlessness, Farrelly also suggested that Turnbull could even *surpass* Menzies, meaning that he'd have to remain in office until 2034 (at the age of 80). To me, it seems like silly conversations at an eastern suburbs journalists' soiree after a few too many drinks has ended up in the pages of a major newspaper. And, unfortunately, presented as serious political journalism.

The old Labor turncoat, former Prime Minister Billy Hughes, remained as a member of Parliament until the age of 90 (he died in office in 1951), but politics today is predominantly not the domain of the aged. To get a picture of decreasing levels of effectiveness in politics, look at Phillip Ruddock now, resembling a walking cadaver, to get an idea of how politics ages people. He's currently 72 and the only reason why he's still in politics is because he hasn't got anything better to do with his time—certainly, his local Amnesty International branch wouldn't be keen to take him in.

Aside from the issue of events that are outside of anyone's control (remembering that although Robert Menzies was Prime Minister for 17 continuous years in his second stint—between 1949 and 1966—he almost lost the 1954 and 1961 elections. John Howard almost lost the 1998 election, and was seriously behind in the polls for most of the 1998–2001 period, before winning the infamous 2001 'Tampa election'), it's impossible to predict what will happen next month in the world of politics, let alone the events of 2027 (or even 2034).

How will the wets–dries dynamic in the Liberal Party play out? Will there be a 2016 Budget before the next election and what will be the outcome of this? What about the hopelessly out-of-depth team behind Turnbull? The Treasurer, Scott Morrison, wouldn't know Budget papers from a Mills & Boon novel, yet he's the one with the finances in his hands. Christian Porter? A wannabe from the West Australia Parliament who has been earmarked as leadership material, but hasn't handled the transition from state to federal politics very well. They might not be competent, but they have grand ambitions to be leader. Ian McFarlane has defected to the National Party—are there any more to come? If Turnbull's ratings plummet, will we see a rerun of the Kevin Rudd disasters?

These are all questions that nobody knows the answers to, except for those sagacious media journalists who believe they hold the fount of all wisdom.

Certainly, Malcolm Turnbull presents as national leader in a way that Tony Abbott never could. We don't feel the cringe or the same embarrassment when Abbott demanded world leaders at the G20 Forum address each other by their first names, or when he gave benign and meaningless economic statements, or endless megaphone-mouthing about 'death cults'. That is a welcome change. But, Turnbull has been in office for less than three months. *Three months!* Aside from a change in what journalists love to call 'atmospherics', there have been no new policies, and all of the much despised agenda from the Abbott government is still in place. Now, that may be removed, but we don't know as yet. Turnbull's leadership was based on the commitment that there would be no change to climate change policy (including the largely wasteful and ineffective Direct Action plan), or to the Liberal Party position on same-sex marriage legislation, which is to hold a national plebiscite to amend the *Marriage Act* (incidentally, a change to the Act to permit same-sex marriage doesn't require a plebiscite and can be amended by a vote in Parliament).

Mainstream journalists have a great national responsibility. Except for the people working closely with political leaders, most electors receive their political information through reporters, journalists and news editors, and form their political opinions through the presentation of this information. The community was badly let down by the media during Tony Abbott's leadership. The man was obviously a foolish leader and totally unsuited to the position of Prime Minister. Despite this, he was supported by friends in the media and largely escaped scrutiny until close to the end of his departure. Turnbull, while he is a vast improvement on Tony Abbott, is still evading the type of scrutiny that inevitably surrounds Labor leaders, most notably during Julia Gillard's tenure. If, Malcolm Turnbull is so clever, why do journalists feel the need to keep pointing this out? So they can acquire this intelligence through osmosis? So that people gloss over his disasters in previous stages of his political career?

And how long will the scrutiny be set aside? Already, the tentacles of the Turnbulls are starting to encroach, much like the Underwoods in the US television series, *House of Cards*. Lucy Turnbull has been appointed as head of the NSW Government's new Greater Sydney Commission. Sure, Lucy Turnbull should be her own woman but, already, we're seeing the overreach of the Turnbulls. There's gushing praise for everything the Turnbulls do, but who will the first journalist with the courage to stand up to them when things start to go wrong? Will they be screamed down, in the same way Dr Hanan Ashrawi was, when she appeared as an obstacle to Malcolm Turnbull's entry into federal Parliament?

I never had a great opinion of Julia Gillard as Prime Minister: I feel that she was in the position before her time and could have been a much greater Prime Minister at a later time, perhaps another two or three years after the point that she actually become Prime Minister in 2010. However, she performed as well as she possibly could under the circumstances of a hung Parliament and I don't think any other contemporary Prime Minister could have survived for as long as she did—certainly not Tony Abbott. Compare the sexist diatribes, personal attacks, and relentless media pressure that Gillard was placed under, with the Hollywood-style fan-fiction kid-glove treatment of Turnbull—the gap is so great that we may as well be comparing reporting that might appear on a subterranean crevice on planet Mars.

In response to a question in 2011 from Channel 7's political reporter Mark Riley about the responsibility of the media and media ethics, Gillard simply responded by suggesting a good starting point would be to "stop writing crap". It can't be any clearer than that.

*

The Turnbull government meandered for the rest of 2015. Riding high in the polls, and the media on tap to report every move in a positive light, Malcolm Turnbull would have expected this to continue into 2016. But momentum is everything in politics and Turnbull became complacent, firing off policy ideas into every direction and expecting the media to run with these ideas, no matter how foolish they seemed. But the public wasn't fooled, and Turnbull's star started to wane from February 2016. Turnbull was surprisingly inarticulate about many things and it seemed that he was not the man the public expected, but a hostage to the conservative wing of the Liberal–National Party.

Day zero and a descent into the maelstrom

26 March 2016

I t's obvious I'm not one of those people that thinks too highly of the Prime Minister, Malcolm Turnbull, and certainly not as highly as many other journalists in the mainstream media. As I've noted elsewhere, there is nothing in Turnbull's political record of note but he continues to be egged on and promoted in the mainstream media, more in the hope that he will do something that justifies his exalted star rating.

The latest in this offering is Fairfax journalist Peter Hartcher's belief that Turnbull's inaction over the past six months has been a cunning plan—Turnbull has been biding his time, not wasting it[1]—and more of the same from the ABC's Annabel Crabb—'The Turnbull of old returns with a DD showdown'[2], where apparently the "PM's manoeuvres over the budget, double dissolution and

1   Peter Hartcher, *Sydney Morning Herald*, 'Weeks in the planning: we now see Malcolm Turnbull has been biding his time, not wasting it', 22 March 2016. http://www.smh.com.au/federal-politics/political-news/weeks-in-the-planning-we-now-see-malcolm-turnbull-has-been-biding-his-time-not-wasting-it-20160321-gnnflt.html

2   Annabel Crabb, ABC News, 'The Turnbull of old returns with a DD showdown', 21 April 2016. http://www.abc.net.au/news/2016-03-21/crabb-the-turnbull-of-old-returns-with-a-dd-showdown/7263536

industrial relations legislation have a familiar Turnbullian feel, and show he has seized the initiative by the scruff of its neck". More opinion dressed up as journalism.

Yesterday (on what is unofficially being considered as the first day of the 2016 election campaign), Turnbull announced he will recall Parliament for three weeks from 18 April, for the Senate to pass the government's contentious legislation to re-introduce the Australian Building and Construction Commission (the Commission that was initiated by the Howard government in 2005, as a gift to future Liberal–National governments to create havoc for the Labor Party and ramp up anti-union rhetoric, with a side-benefit of slightly reducing a small amount of corruption in the building and construction industry). A greater benefit to the community would be creating a national corruption commission, which could look at not only corruption in the building and construction industry, but also look into all types of white collar crime, such as scandals at Comminsure[3] and the Commonwealth Bank of Australia[4] (where people's savings disappeared through poor financial advice and legitimate insurance payouts were denied), as well as investigating corruption within politics.[5] Aside from the possibility of sweeping up many politicians from all sides of politics, it's difficult to see why a national corruption commission hasn't been floated by either of the main parties, as it's sure to be a favourite with the electorate.

Strictly speaking, Turnbull's plan to recall Parliament is not a 'decision' but more like the start of a campaign to set up a process to

---

3   Sarah Danckert, *Sydney Morning Herald*, 'ASA calls for royal commission in wake of CommInsure scandal', 10 March 2016. http://www.smh.com.au/business/banking-and-finance/asa-calls-for-royal-commission-in-wake-of-comminsure-scandal-20160310-gnfbtn.html

4   John Dagge, *Herald Sun*, 'Commonwealth Bank clients strike back over financial planning scandal', 12 October 2014. http://www.heraldsun.com.au/business/commonwealth-bank-clients-strike-back-over-financial-planning-scandal/news-story/f563d297442567d665d93b7836be3c99

5   Jamelle Wells, ABC News, 'Arthur Sinodinos defends $200,000 salary at ICAC inquiry into Australian Water Holdings', 3 April 2014. http://www.abc.net.au/news/2014-04-03/sinodinos-to-give-evidence-at-icac-inquiry-into-awh/5363408

commence the pathway to an election on 2 July. It's not a decision, in the true sense of the word, but that hasn't stopped the lathering up in the media—Turnbull's leadership has been so weak since he became Prime Minister in September 2015 that any microscopic evidence of decisiveness is lauded as a major achievement, and a true sign that the anointed leader has arrived.

This weakness has been evident in Turnbull completely reneging his stances on the Australian Republic, same-sex marriage, climate change (issues which, as far as the public are concerned, are those that define Turnbull), more recently, supporting the campaign by the extreme right of the Liberal–National Party to remove the federally funded Safe Schools program (which, incidentally was funded by Tony Abbott when he was Prime Minister, and received a relatively small amount of $8 million).

But the prime evidence of his weakness has been a lack of action over the past six months since he became Prime Minister.

If Turnbull was a strong leader, minutes after attaining the prime ministership, he would have double-crossed those in the party that supported him, create a reign of terror in the party and threaten the preselection of anyone that spoke out against him or any of his policies, implemented a timetable for the republic, cancelled the Coalition's Direct Action program and created an emissions trading scheme, and brought on a bill to enact same-sex marriage legislation. Why? Because that's what the public expected him to get on with, and that's why his popularity rocketed when he became Prime Minister.

A strong leader would have then talked about the broad brushes of economic reform and tax policy throughout the rest of September and early October, and then, capitalising on his stratospheric popularity at the time, called a lower-house election in late October and held the election on 28 November 2015. He might have achieved a solid mandate, new-found authority, government guaranteed for another three years and any complicated separate Senate elections dealt with in the future.

But Malcolm Turnbull is not a strong political leader. What

might have worked for him in business, is not working politically—
the electorate is many steps ahead of the mainstream media and
have worked out Turnbull's flaws for themselves, as can be seen
with Turnbull's drop in approval ratings to negative territory,[6] and
the latest Morgan Poll[7] showing a LNP 49.5 per cent/ALP 51.5
per cent split.

Instead of strong leadership, we've had waffling and dithering
leadership, confusion over tax policy and financial matters from
Treasurer Scott Morrison (who, surely, must be the weakest
Treasurer since Labor's John Kerrin in 1991), and few policy
announcements (aside from the 'Welcome to the Ideas Boom',[8]
which is more of an 'agenda' than a policy of substance, brought to
you courtesy of a $28 million government advertising campaign).

Instead of the supposed 'respecting the intelligence of the
electorate' and debating the contest of economic ideas, Turnbull
slid into the mud ring with a hysterical and unhinged attack on
Labor's negative gearing policy announcement[9] (joined in by
Minister for Immigration Peter Dutton, claiming "the economy
will come to a shuddering halt and... the stock market will
crash"[10]). So, no one's intelligence ended up being respected and
we ended up back at what resembled the first day of Politics 101
on a university campus.

And here is Turnbull's greatest problem. Although he didn't

6   Phillip Hudson, *The Australian*, 'Newspoll: Malcolm Turnbull's approval into negative
    territory, still trusted over Bill Shorten', 21 March 2016. http://www.theaustralian.com.
    au/national-affairs/newspoll-malcolm-turnbulls-approval-into-negative-territory-still-
    trusted-over-bill-shorten/news-story/7b34b25c10e42af83faf9d4a7195d03a

7   Roy Morgan Research, 'ALP & L-NP now too close to call as electors react to
    Government forcing Senate voting changes last week as Turnbull today recalls
    Parliament in April for Double Dissolution Election showdown', 21 March 2016.
    http://www.roymorgan.com/findings/6723-morgan-poll-federal-voting-intention-
    march-21-2016-201603210505

8   Australian Government, National Innovation & Science Agenda. http://www.innovation.
    gov.au

9   Australian Labor Party, 'Positive plan to help housing affordability'. http://www.alp.org.
    au/negativegearing

10 Dan Conifer, ABC News, 'Peter Dutton says economy will 'come to a shuddering halt'
    under Labor's tax policies', 9 March 2016. http://www.abc.net.au/news/2016-03-09/
    dutton-says-stock-market-will-crash-under-labor's-tax-policies/7233864

specifically announce it, there was an expectation that Malcolm Turnbull, in the electorate's eye, would be different, almost like the 'non-politician' politician, someone who could be different, and move the country to a new place after the divisive and disastrous days of Tony Abbott.

His rhetoric is right—his statements about innovation, agility were hitting the right tone and chords with the media—but there's a dissonance between expectations (mainly heightened by the media) and reality. And now the government has been caught up with the esoteric issues of Senate reform, speculation about double dissolution elections, and trying to explain intricate issues contained in Section 57 of the Constitution. These are classic insider conversations.

I really dislike the idea of the 'pub test' but you wouldn't even need to go to the pub to realise very few people are seriously interested in Senate reform legislation and even less are concerned about what a double dissolution election is. But the more the speculation goes on (as well as the schisms within the Liberal–National Party between the Turnbull and Abbott camps), it keeps on sending out the message that the government is purely concerned about its own interests and not those of the electorate. And nobody in the Labor Party would need to be reminded about what the disastrous electorate consequences of this can be (well, I'll remind them again—it results in a loss of 17 seats, a loss of government and at least two terms on the Opposition benches).

Turnbull can turn this around—although the Turnbull government has done very little in six months, and the fact that the polls are showing that we're in hung-Parliament territory, it is not disastrous for him. But the strategy all seems so wrong. It seems that there won't be any tax policy announcement until the Budget is announced on 3 May—giving Labor about five weeks of time to make grand policy announcements, while Turnbull and Morrison can only keep suggesting that people should wait until 3 May before they hear any major announcements from the Liberals.

And then what happens? What will happen after 3 May? The level of expectation will be dramatic—what if the Budget is poorly received? Or if the tax policy is not perceived to be a tax policy at all? A Budget reply by Bill Shorten on 5 May, and then the announcement on 6 May that a double dissolution election will be held on 2 July? Shorten will start the campaign with all the momentum.

And, of top of this, an eight-week campaign! Turnbull's leadership is on the verge of the downward death spiral, where leadership perceptions become fixed and, irrespective of how many supporters in the media the Prime Minister might have, become too difficult to budge (as John Howard discovered during the 2007 election campaign).

What will Turnbull talk about between now and the Budget on 3 May? What can he do to reverse the downward trend in his leadership and party numbers? For Turnbull's sake, and the Liberals, it will need to be an excellent Budget. And an even better election campaign, that is, if anyone is left standing or listening.

*

National opinion polls up to 26 March 2016

Morgan, 12–13, 19–20 Mar 2016
LNP 49.5% | ALP 50.5%

Newspoll, 17–20 Mar 2016
LNP 51% | ALP 49%

Ipsos, 10–12 Mar 2016
LNP 53% | ALP 47%

Newspoll, 3–6 Mar 2016
LNP 50% | ALP 50%

Essential, 2–6 Mar 2016
LNP 50% | ALP 50%

Betting as at 26 March 2016

LNP $1.20
ALP $4.50

Prediction as at 26 March 2016

Too close to call, although other more learned pundits such as psephologist Peter Brent are suggesting a strong Liberal–National Coalition victory, holding onto 85 seats[11] out of 150 seats (or a loss of five seats).

11   Peter Brent, *Inside Story*, 'How Turnbull-in-freefall became Malcolm the strategic genius', 22 March 2016. http://insidestory.org.au/how-turnbull-in-freefall-became-malcolm-the-strategic-genius

A Coalition masterclass on how to lose an election

30 April 2016

I t's not always the best strategy that wins elections, but it certainly does help to get the best pack of political cards together, keep them close to your chest, and go all out to win the campaign. Sometimes, unorthodox tactics can work. Sometimes, clever manoeuvres can confuse opponents and deliver success. Making noise through the media can also work, as well as tactics such as recalling Parliament for three whole weeks,[1] and stand-over threats to the Senate to pass unpalatable legislation, or else be faced with a double dissolution election. And it also helps to be ahead in the polls.

But what to do if none of these plans are working, and the result of all of these bizarre political tactics results in your party falling behind in the polls?[2] And only six months after installing a popular leader that was expected to trounce the Opposition at the forthcoming election?

1   Matthew Knott, *Sydney Morning Herald*, 'Malcolm Turnbull recalls Parliament for April 18 sitting ahead of early election', 21 March 2016. http://www.smh.com.au/federal-politics/political-news/malcolm-turnbull-recalls-parliament-for-april-18-sitting-ahead-of-early-election-20160320-gnmy2v.html
2   News.com.au, 'Close result predicted for election: poll', 18 April 2016. http://www.news.com.au/finance/work/leaders/close-result-predicted-for -election-poll/news-story/70b2 7b30d4cb7169f292611452c709c9

I've been watching politics for a long time, and it's difficult to imagine a more incoherent, unstable, and disunified government heading into an election campaign, where messaging is sporadic, low-order issues are being magnified but remain low-order issues, and higher-order issues are being ignored or dismissed.

It's also difficult to remember when a first-term government seeking re-election had so little to offer the electorate, either when reflecting on any past achievements, or seeking a platform for future plans and policies for consideration by the electorate.

Although I disagree with a reinstallation of the Australian Building and Construction Commission in the proposed format, behind the confected outrage put forward by the Prime Minister, Malcolm Turnbull, and senior Coalition figures, it's possible to see what the strategy is—rabbit on to the community about union corruption and building corruption reducing 20 per cent of national productivity[3] (this erroneous claim was made by Independent Economics—so independent that they're also independent from fact—and was widely discredited, and the report eventually removed from the ABCC's website)—then make unreasonable demands of the Senate to pass unconscionable legislation and, there you have it: a trigger to hold a double dissolution election, a compliant Governor–General, and the electorate primed to swallow the misinformation during an election campaign.

However misguided the strategy is (only 18 per cent of people support the reintroduction of the ABCC[4] and even fewer understand what it actually is), we can still see what the strategy is. But the recent plans to abolish the Road Safety Remuneration Tribunal? Well, that's something that's arrived from a deep hole

---

3   Peter Martin, *Sydney Morning Herald*, 'Restoring the ABCC a poor foundation for Malcolm Turnbull to build an election on', 24 March 2016. http://www.smh.com.au/comment/restoring-the-abcc-a-poor-foundation-for -malcolm-turnbull-to-build-an-election-on-20160322-gnox7n.html

4   Sabra Lane, ABC Television, *7.30*, 'Nearly half of all voters have no opinion on double dissolution election: poll', 22 March 2016. http://www.abc.net.au/news/2016-03-22/double-dissolution-voters-opinion-election-survey/7266096

in the ground, and will be provided in future MBA and political science courses as examples for how not to produce a successful political campaign—not up there with Germany's venture into Stalingrad during World War II, but certainly hovering nearby.

First of all, the Road Safety Remuneration Tribunal was created as a result of very strong evidence that there is a causal link between driver renumeration and truck accidents on major transport routes around Australia.[5] While transport road safety is an important issue for the community, and steps to reduce trucking accidents should be taken, the RSR Tribunal is a low-order issue for many in the electorate, and to make it an election platform issue is a serious mistake, and difficult to understand the rationale behind the Coalition's tactics.

A subsequent rally in Canberra, promoted by an astroturfed lobby group supported by the Institute of Public Affairs, had all the hallmarks of an *ad hoc* disorganised campaign. Having the Prime Minister of the day attending such a rally (and I'm being generous calling it a rally—there were only around 50 people in attendance) was a mistake.

Squint a little at the vision shown on television and online, and the 'mums and dads driver owner' rally look similar to the 'axe the tax' rallies organised by then Leader of the Opposition, Tony Abbott in 2012. But no need to squint to realise Sophie Mirabella appeared at both rallies. *Sophie Mirabella!*

Why the Liberal strategy team decided that the Prime Minister of the day should appear with a tossed-out former member of Parliament seeking to regain the Victorian seat of Indi, alongside the bizarre sight of Minister for Employment, Michaelia Cash, screeching in overdrive, is hard to fathom. Prime Ministers are meant to be above this riff-raff: better to leave this sort of action to a Treasurer, or other parliamentary underlings.

....

5   National Transport Commission, 'Heavy Vehicle Compliance Review, Consultation Draft, September 2013'. https://www.ntc.gov.au/Media/Reports/(3B77B568-8930-B2FD-3075-22B4C35D05E7).pdf

And, politics being the way it is, now the issue has blown away, with the public even less aware about what the RSR Tribunal is, and the Prime Minister was seen to lose control over an issue the electorate doesn't really care about.

Alongside this, the Senate refused to pass the Coalition's ABCC legislation, giving Malcolm Turnbull his 'trigger' to call a double dissolution election. But the big problem for Turnbull was the Senate only took one day to block the ABCC legislation—Parliament was no longer needed for the allocated three weeks, and the Prime Minister was left with a political vacuum which, of course, needed to be filled.

What followed is instructive for how unsuited and unprepared Malcolm Turnbull is for the prime ministership. After weeks of hectoring the Senate to 'make a quick decision[6]' on these bills, when the decision arrived—quickly, as the Prime Minister had demanded—he was left with nothing to talk about. Nothing!

Without an agenda to pursue in Parliament, Turnbull went out to the public: a photo opportunity with the Mignaccas, an aspirational family in the southern Sydney suburb of Penshurst, to discuss the benefits of the Liberal–National Party negative gearing policy.[7] There are different levels of disasters in politics, but this one gets a high score of around nine out of ten. As it turns out, this negatively-geared family was bemoaning Labor's idea of restrictions to negative gearing policies on housing, in that it would restrict their potential to buy a house (incidentally, their third negatively geared house) for their one-year old toddler. *Their one-year-old toddler!*

Turnbull and his Treasurer, Scott Morrison, proceeded with the mother-of-all-scare-campaigns and one was definitely left

6   Shalailah Medhora, *The Guardian*, 'Malcolm Turnbull urges 'quick decision' on bills as double-dissolution inches closer', 17 April 2016. http://www.theguardian.com/australia-news/2016/apr/17/malcolm-turnbull-urges-quick-decision-on-bills-as-double-dissolution-inches-closer

7   Charis Chang, News.com.au, 'Malcolm Turnbull's photo call with suburban family backfires', 26 April 2016. http://www.news.com.au/finance/economy/australian-economy/malcolm-turnbulls-photo-call-with-suburban-family-backfires/news-story/eff9e413d5e22467f5a006551671cc35

with the impression that Labor's policy, if implemented, will cause earthquakes, famine, the Bubonic plague, the first born of every parent offered to ancient Gods for blood sacrifice, and the collapse of the pillars of society. If only their response was a bit more, shall we say, *nuanced*, there's a better chance that the electorate would take these propositions a little bit more seriously.

What these flusterings masked was the fact that the top ten electorates that negatively gear around Australia are all Liberal-held electorates, with Turnbull's own seat, Wentworth, topping the list—the average claim on negative gearing through the tax system is over $19,000 in the seat of Wentworth.

So, who should we believe, the politician or the expert? I'd go with the expert.

The Grattan Institute responded by saying that there were many flaws in the argument presented by the Coalition[8], and that far from being the 'mums and dads' investors that benefit, it is mainly higher-income earners that use negative gearing to reduce their tax burden.[9] This seems like a no-win argument that's being presented by Turnbull, so why does he persist?

Turnbull outdid himself on ABC's *7.30*: the level of dexterity was low, and as far political disasters are concerned, this is probably as bad as it gets.[10] This interview with Leigh Sales was possibly the worst political performance by a sitting Prime Minister.[11] There's bluster, there's bluff, there's mansplaining, there's condescension, and a performance that showed that Turnbull was totally unprepared and unbriefed.

8   Macrobusiness, 'Grattan annihilates Turnbull negative gearing lies…again', 27 April 2016. http://www.macrobusiness.com.au/2016/04/grattan-annhilates-turnbull-negative-lies-again

9   Peter Martin, *Sydney Morning Herald*, 'Federal budget 2016: Top earners benefit most from negative gearing, Grattan Institute finds', 25 April 2016. http://www.smh.com.au/business/federal-budget/federal-budget-2016-top-earners-benefit-most-from-negative-gearing-grattan-institute-finds-20160425-goeef5.html

10 ABC Television, *7.30*, 'Negative gearing & capital gains: Turnbull says high earners make highest gains' via YouTube, 26 April 2016. https://youtu.be/QDb1hAK0Rjc

11 ABC Television, *7.30*, 'Interview: Malcolm Turnbull', 26 April 2016. http://www.abc.net.au/7.30/content/2015/s4450761.htm

When asked by Leigh Sales for evidence he had to support his claim that 30 per cent of investors would flee from the housing market if Labor's proposed reforms to negative gearing rules were introduced, he said that it was 'a matter of common sense'. Any other Prime Minister would have had figures at hand (even if they were factually incorrect) but Turnbull just stated his 'common sense' argument, echoing the same logic used by Pauline Hanson[12] and the famous 'Lambassador', Sam Kekovich. This is not good company to be associated with in politics, unless your affiliations are closer to Reclaim Australia or the United Patriotic Front.

So, where to for the Coalition? The 2016 Budget is next Tuesday, but expectations about what it will achieve are so low, that the Coalition can hardly be expected to receive a boost from it—bracket creep (where salary increases through inflation push wage earners into a higher tax scale) seems to be where the Coalition wants to limit itself to, and that's not exactly the type of issue the commentariat or the public are likely to get excited about. And, Malcolm Turnbull has painted himself so far into a corner, that's it difficult to see how the Budget would rescue Turnbull from his underwhelming performances.

The issues that could potentially be positives for Turnbull—climate change, Republicanism, same-sex marriage, education funding, health, technology, the economy—have all been removed from Turnbull... by Turnbull. He's junked the issues that the electorate perceives to be the strengths of Malcolm Turnbull. He appears unprepared and, as I've mentioned before, has nothing in his political history to suggest that anything will improve. Even the 'Ideas Boom' has blown up in his face: it's an 'agenda' littered with digital motherhood statements and thought bubbles.[13] And ideas such as the 30-minute cities[14]

12   One Nation, 'A Special Message From Pauline Hanson', 19 November 2014. http://
      www.onenation.com.au/current_affairs/a-special-message-from-pauline-hanson
13   Australian Government, National Innovation & Science Agenda. http://www.innovation.
      gov.au
14   James Massola & Peter Martin, *Sydney Morning Herald*, 'Malcolm Turnbull to borrow big in

and the very-fast-train between Sydney and Melbourne just continue with the thought bubble processes—these are 50-year plans that need co-ordination and detailed planning with the States and Territories, and not just foisted upon the electorate weeks before an election campaign.

The latest Essential Poll shows LNP 48 per cent/ALP 52 per cent of the two-party preferred vote. This is at an election-losing level for the Liberal–National Coalition, and eight weeks before the supposed election on 2 July, it's not looking good for Malcolm Turnbull. Governments can recover from this position during an election campaign but, if the campaign looks anything like the past two months, the Coalition is in for a shocking time in the lead up to election.

*

Polls up to 30 April 2016

Essential, 20–24 Apr 2016
LNP 48% | ALP 52%

Newspoll, 14–17 Apr 2016
LNP 49% | ALP 51%

Essential, 13–17 Apr 2016
LNP 50% | ALP 50%

Morgan, 9–10, 16–17 Apr 2016
LNP 50% | ALP 50%

Ipsos, 14–16 Apr 2016
LNP 50% | ALP 50%

multibillion-dollar cities plan', 29 April 2016. http://www.smh.com.au/federal-politics/federal-election-2016/malcolm-turnbull-to-borrow-big-in-multibilliondollar-smart-cities-plan-20160428-gohbym.html

ReachTEL, 14 Apr 2016
LNP 50% | ALP 50%

Essential, 6–10 Apr 2016
LNP 50% | ALP 50%

Betting as at 30 April 2016

LNP $1.34
ALP $3.25

Prediction as at 30 April 2016

I've always maintained that incumbency usually adds a great benefit to a government during election campaigns, but the Liberal–National Coalition has been behaving too poorly to take great advantage of this. It has also telegraphed it's intention to hold the election on 2 July before officially announcing it, so that's one less issue for Labor to worry about.

The margin of 19 seats is a great barrier to a Labor victory. Having said that, current polling suggests a narrow Labor victory. Seats in Queensland will be critical and if a swing against the government of around 4 per cent is achieved in NSW, it will be very close election. Now that Malcolm Turnbull is quickly becoming as ineffective as Tony Abbott, the experience of the Liberal–National Party losing the Queensland election in 2015 is becoming instructive, as is the Coalition's loss in the election in Victoria in 2014 (as well as the 10 per cent swing to Labor during the 2015 NSW election).

Nick Economou from Monash University, believes the Coalition will be returned with a much reduced majority.[15] I think it will be much closer than that.

....

15 Nick Economou, *The Conversation*, State by state, it's still Malcolm Turnbull's election to lose', 28 April 2016. http://theconversation.com/state-by-state-its-still-malcolm-turnbulls-election-to-lose-58047

Turnbull lets everyone know that he's on the ropes

11 May 2016

For all those fans of chess out there, they'd understand that there's a strong correlation between the game and the military. All those tactics and strategies, deciding when to take the bishop or the rook, skillful trickery and gamesmanship, giving up a seemingly valuable piece to gain advantage and knowing when to offer up a few pawns, all in the name of achieving the checkmate, or the battle victory.

Election campaigns are similar to chess too, but with Prime Minister Malcolm Turnbull announcing a 54-day lead up to the election on 2 July, the 2016 campaign will be more like a three-layered chessboard, with diabolical Sudokus and the Times Crossword thrown in for good measure. It will be complicated and, because we're in relatively new territory as far as campaign longevity is concerned, it's difficult to know who will benefit from this. But, just like it is in chess, it will be the nuanced campaigner that wins; the player that knows which move to make and when, and which tactics will deceive and trick their opponent.

Only one-third of the election campaign has been completed so far, but there are very worrying signs for the Liberal–National Coalition (not that the Labor campaign has been without problems) and, if things continue in the way they are going at the moment, the voters in Wentworth might be looking at a by-election in the latter part of the year, after their local member, Malcolm Turnbull, retires from politics because of his party's loss at the 2016 election.

You just know that things are going bad for a government when they start to highlight personalities at the expense of good policy, and extend that to making their own brand name invisible.

The Liberal–National Party has unveiled a new look—'The Turnbull Coalition Team', with no reference to the Liberal Party, or the National Party, and no logo. It's part *The West Wing*, it's part US Presidential and, you could argue, part pantomime, part comedy. Of course, the new look confirms that 'brand Liberal' is like a bucket of poison in the electorate and telegraphs this confirmation, not just to the electorate, but the strategists at Labor Party headquarters—the big dollars they've paid to Essential Media to qualitatively research what the Liberals' 'brand' means to the community have been verified—by the Liberal Party.

And you can bet your eighth negatively-geared house (if you are lucky enough to have one, or if you're a Liberal member of Parliament) that over the next 54 days, Labor will be referring to 'the Turnbull Liberal government' at every opportunity, linking the electoral poison with about the only thing the Liberals have going for them, a quickly diminishing Malcolm Turnbull.

This tactic of removing political party branding from candidates is a relatively new one—it was first used by former Labor Prime Minister Paul Keating in the 1996 election—but every party that has used it on a large-scale level, whether it be state or federal, has lost the election. The message that it sends to the electorate is two-fold: the party is so weak that it's not worth voting for, and even its own candidates don't believe in it. Sure, it might be subliminal, but it's a net negative. In chess, it's a bit like opening with the Sicilian defense but then realising that all of your pawns are missing.

Still, we're waiting for an advance from 'boats', and 'negative gearing', the only two main issues that Malcolm Turnbull and the Liberals have talked about so far. And they've brought out the megaphone on the supposed threat of a Greens–Labor coalition in case of another minority government, even though the chances of this happening are very slim, either the hung Parliament, or a Greens–Labor coalition.

But the moment for me which indicates how badly the Liberal–National Coalition is travelling, and how difficult it will be for them to claw back, was the appearance of Kelly O'Dwyer and Innes Willox on Monday night's episode of the ABC's *Q&A*. If you'd ever want to see two public figures that are so out of touch with the ways of the world, it was an episode not to be missed. It was O'Dwyer, Minister for Small Business and Assistant Treasurer, and Willox, head of the Australian Industry Group and former chief-of-staff to former Minister for Foreign Affairs, Alexander Downer, up against Duncan Storrar from the *Q&A* audience, a 45-year-old father, with low employment skills, a low income, and a history of mental illnesses.

A simple question from Storrar: why do people like him receive nothing from Budget 2016, but a person earning $1,000,000 receives a tax break of $16,715.[1]

O'Dwyer patronised about the dubious supply-side economics argument of the 1980s 'growing the pie' (the 1980s are *so yesterday!*), and Willox interrogated him about the amount of tax that he pays, surmising that Storrar pays GST, "just like the rest of us". It was the moment that emphasises the gap between Coalition policy, and the lives lived in the suburbs. O'Dwyer and Willox reeked of the exclusive private school education that they come from, having probably never understood what it's like to be unemployed and never short of cash or life opportunities.

---

1   Michael Lallo, *Sydney Morning Herald*, 'Media failed Duncan Storrar, and the issues he's raised', 14 May 2016. http://www.smh.com.au/entertainment/tv-and-radio/media-failed-duncan-storrar-and-the-issues-he-raised-20160514-gov5ig.html

The Leader of the Opposition, Bill Shorten, also had his troubles, with border security again being the big issue that Minister for Immigration, Peter Dutton, is exploiting to its fullest, trawling through the internet to find any evidence at all of current Labor candidates offering any skerrick of antagonism to the Coalition's boat turn-back policy (real or imagined). Evidently, the Liberal Party has decided the Australian public is more interested in a small amount of people seeking asylum by boat, than cost of living issues, the future of education, childcare, health, and whether there'll be any jobs for them in Malcolm Turnbull's new economy of innovation.

In the same manner that state election campaigns predictably focus upon 'law and order', the Coalition is focusing on asylum seekers, and it's only a matter of time before terrorism and Islam enters the campaign. It's just a question of which Minister is allocated the task of introducing this as a campaign issue.

Will it work? Contrary to the common perception that negative campaigning works, the electorate prefers a positive message. The Coalition is currently losing the campaign because, alongside Malcolm Turnbull sounding bored in his interactions with the public on the hustings, its messaging is incoherent, it sounds desperate, it has decided to trash its own brand, and by focusing on asylum seekers and terrorism, it sends out the obvious message that it has nothing to offer the electorate.

*

Polls up to 11 May 2016

Newspoll, 5–8 May 2016
LNP 49% | ALP 51%

Ipsos, 5–7 May 2016
LNP 51% | ALP 49%

Galaxy, 4–6 May 2016
LNP 50% | ALP 50%

ReachTEL, 5 May 2016
LNP 50% | ALP 50%

Essential, 27 Apr–1 May 2016
LNP 48% | ALP 52%

Morgan, 23–24, 30 Apr–1 May 2016
LNP 49% | ALP 51%

Betting as at 11 May 2016

LNP $1.26
ALP $3.70

Prediction as at 11 May 2016

Although this is not reflected in the betting, Labor is currently in a position to claim a narrow victory, possibly a narrow win by two seats. Depending on how many independent or Green candidates claim a seat, a minority government is also a possibility, although unlikely.

Malcolm Turnbull and his disappearance act

28 May 2016

The election campaign has now moved to overdrive, even though there are still another five weeks to go. Following my previous correspondence, I was ridiculed for comparing politics and the election campaign with the game of chess, so I'll now make a more suitable comparison with the video game, *Call Of Duty: Ghosts*, where sniper rifles, machine guns and rocket launchers are released, aliens and the Kraken appear alongside acid-flinging scorpions, shark attacks, and mutually assured destruction is achieved in the Extinction mode. That's probably a better indication of how the next five weeks will proceed.

The fun and games in real life commenced towards the end of last week, when the Australian Federal Police decided that an election campaign is the best time to raid the offices of the Labor Party and their staffers in Melbourne, in the search for leaks coming from NBN Co., the government-owned company responsible for rolling out the Coalition's much derided multi-technology-mix broadband internet.[1] It might have been better

---

1   Renai LeMay, *DeLimiter*, 'Australia's broadband ranking dive shows MTM right for NBN, says Fifield', 4 April 2016. https://delimiter.com.au/2016/04/04/australias-broadband-

for the AFP to actually investigate the source of leaks—NBN Co.—but that's not going to produce the type of damaging headlines to prop up the Liberal–National Party, so best to raid the offices of your political opponents and... *surprise!* ...take photographs of Labor's communications policies, and distribute to your work colleagues.

The Prime Minister, Malcolm Turnbull, denied too much for my liking. He over-egged his case that the AFP is an independent organisation with its own free will, and claimed 'it is entirely fanciful' that he or his government would direct the AFP to raid the offices of his opponents (well, that's what US President Richard Nixon also claimed during the Watergate scandal in the 1970s). Of course, raiding your opponent's offices to besmirch their reputation is a tactic straight out of the US Republican dirt handbook (incidentally, where the Liberals' campaign strategist, Mark Textor, learned all the skills of the dark political arts).

Andrew Colvin, the Commissioner of the Australian Federal Police, also came in to lend a hand, saying that the AFP is 'totally independent of the government', and the Prime Minister and government knew nothing about the raids (a claim that was subsequently contradicted by Minister for Communications, Mitch Fifield). Conveniently, Turnbull then conflated national security issues with an allegation that Labor had "stolen documents" (how would he know they were "stolen" if, as he claimed, he didn't know anything about the raids?). I recall that former Prime Minister, Tony Abbott, was bedding at the headquarters of the AFP in Canberra for almost two years—I don't think it was just for pyjama parties and gingerbread suppers, so any suggestion the AFP wouldn't do whatever they can to support their side of politics is not credible.

The AFP raids followed the dog-whistling from Minister for Immigration, Peter Dutton on Sky News, where he said refugees are illiterate and innumerate[2] and have this magical

---

ranking-dive-shows-mtm-right-nbn-says-fifield

2   Latika Bourke, *Sydney Morning Herald*, 'Peter Dutton says 'illiterate and innumerate''

skill of simultaneously being unemployed, and taking the jobs that would normally be fulfilled by Australians (which, to my knowledge, are the jobs that many Australians aren't keen to take up—unskilled, manual labour, shopping trolley collection, cleaning, caring of the aged).

But, of course, the purpose of this behaviour from a Minister is not to be coherent, but to pander to the clichés about refugees and asylum seekers—and applying three-fold messaging to swinging votes: refugees are a drain on the public purse, they're stealing Australian jobs, and they're idle people that are happy to loaf about on unemployment benefits. Will this tactic work? We'll look at this later on.

The trifecta of political nonsense was completed when Treasurer, Scott Morrison, and Minister for Finance, Mathias Cormann, teamed up to provide a bizarre vaudeville of folksy foolishness, mistruths and meaningless graphs on sandwich boards, claiming that Labor's election figures have a '$67 billion black hole'. The purpose of this, again, is not logic (admitted by Morrison when he said his strategy was about 'flushing Labor out') or gain the approval of any sensible economist, but to get the headline figure in the media—even if Morrison and Cormann were made to look foolish, and lightly taken to task by at least some in the mainstream media.

I thought that might be enough for one week, but then National Party Leader and Deputy Prime Minister Barnaby Joyce decided to make the link between Labor's decision to suspend live export trade to Indonesia in 2011[3] and the immediate increase in asylum seekers arriving in Australia by boat, suggesting that Indonesia deliberately forced refugees

refugees would take Australian jobs', 18 May 2016. http://www.smh.com.au/federal-politics/federal-election-2016/peter-dutton-says-illiterate-and-innumerate-refugees-would-take-australian-jobs-20160517-goxhj1.html

3   Matthew Doran & Samantha Hawley, ABC News, 'Barnaby Joyce suggests asylum seeker boat influx under Labor coincided with live export halt', 26 May 2016. http://www.abc.net.au/news/2016-05-25/asylum-seeker-influx-coincided-with-live-ex-halt-joyce-suggests/7446456

across the seas to Australia. It's an inflammatory remark—it's the type of loose remark that commences wars—but Turnbull shrugged it off, saying "there is no link between the Indonesian government and people smuggling". And that was the end of that.

Racism, sloganeering, mistruths, bigotry, all coming from the mouths of his Ministers—so much for Malcolm Turnbull's rhetoric about "treating the electorate with the respect they deserve" and respecting the electorate's intelligence. If what the Liberal–National Party has offered over the past three weeks is an indication, then it's very obvious Turnbull (and the newly-minted 'Turnbull Coalition Team') has a very low opinion of the electorate's intelligence, and has no intention of offering any respect.

And what does the electorate think of this so far? It's Day 19 of this extended election campaign, but this would be Day 1 in a usual 35-day campaign, so it difficult to know how engaged the electorate is. What has happened so far has mainly been shadow boxing, and claim and counter-claim from all sides of politics, trying to win the daily tactics and negate an opponent's messaging. However, the issue that frequently arises in many conversations in Malcolm Turnbull himself.

While manning the phones and speaking with voters at our local candidate's office, every conversation focused around the 'disappointment' that many felt about Malcolm Turnbull since he become Prime Minister—it's not anger, but the disappointment is obvious. *'He's not what he said he would be'* says one Liberal voter—even though Turnbull never specifically said what 'he would be' on the day he became Prime Minister—but I guess this is based on the perception of Turnbull's history: his support for progressive issues, such as the Republic, an advocate for climate change policy, same-sex marriage. But he definitely did state that he would respect the intelligence of the electorate, and we're still waiting for this to happen.

And the more Turnbull gets into the muck and the dirt (the

AFP raids, condoning an openly racist Minister for Immigration by proclaiming that he is an "outstanding minister", when he is obviously not; supporting a clearly incompetent Deputy Prime Minister; the empty rhetoric and florid statements; slogans—referring to Bill Shorten as "billion dollar Bill"—maniacal and hysterical attacks on everything Labor), the more he disappoints. It wasn't meant to be like this.

Another voter on the phone, this one a swinging voter: *"I thought that he would be different, but he's just like all the others"*. Turnbull's personal approval ratings have nose-dived, and his net approval rating is exactly the same as Leader of the Opposition, Bill Shorten: minus 12.

Of the past 23 published opinion polls, the Liberal–National Party has been ahead in only two: the Labor Party has been ahead in 11 polls, and the other 10 have been even at 50:50. The current ReachTEL poll has the nation-wide two-party preferred vote sitting at 52 per cent for Labor, and 48 per cent for the LNP. Although the Liberal–National Party is still in the box seat (incumbency, continuous favourable coverage in all mainstream media, especially from the ABC, and a margin of 21 seats, are difficult obstacles for an Opposition to overcome), these are not great numbers.

Of course, being this far out from the election day on 2 July, there are so many factors that will come into play. And, my insider information (I'm not *that* type of insider, but a bit of an outsider–insider) shows that polling for key marginal seats is not that good for the Labor, and not so great for Tony Windsor, running against Barnaby Joyce in the seat of New England—leading me to think that there will be major seat gains for the Labor Party, but not from the expected locations.

There have also been recent comparisons put out by the Liberals about the 2015 UK Election[4], where Labour's leader

4   Tom McIlroy, *Sydney Morning Herald*, 'Election 2016: Scott Morrison downplays opinion poll pointing to Labor victory', 23 May 2016. http://www.smh.com.au/federal-politics/federal-election-2016/election-2016-scott-morrison-downplays-opinion-poll-pointing-to-

Ed Milliband was favoured in the polls to win the election but, instead, the electorate swung strongly behind the Conservatives on election day, and re-elected David Cameron as UK Prime Minister. However, there are no comparisons between the performance of the UK Conservatives, and the Liberal–National Party, where the LNP has been riven by internal divisions, they removed the incumbent Prime Minister, Tony Abbott, and, generally, they've been a poorly performing government.

The performance of the Liberal–National Party since their election in September 2013 has generally been one of ideological navel gazing and incompetence, firstly under Tony Abbott, and a high dose of nothingness under Malcolm Turnbull since September 2015. Nothing has been achieved, and there is no platform for re-election.

The 'vibe' has changed for the Liberal–National Party: their body language and hysterical over-egging of outrageous political statements suggests their internal polling is on the verge of some kind of disaster. No doubt, there will be other political tricks to play with—Mark Textor is prepared to go to the deep dark recesses of the human psyche to gain political advantage, so who knows where this will end up.

However, the pollsters Crosby–Textor text book doesn't always work; proof can be found in the 2016 London mayoral election. Employed by the Conservatives, Crosby–Textor used Islamophobia to discredit Labour's candidate, Sadiq Khan, and created spurious links with terrorism. After this attack, Khan's personal support improved, and he won the final vote by 57–43 per cent. The London electorate saw through these tactics, but will the Australian electorate do the same?

There are signs that they can. When Barnaby Joyce made his ill-informed comments on ABC's *Q&A* linking live export trade with asylum seeker boats, there was a collection groan in the live television audience, the type of groan that asks: *We've seen these tricks before and they are so 2001! Show us something new!*

But the best moment of the campaign so far comes from the south-coast NSW town of Eden, where Indigenous elder, Pastor Ossie Cruse, performed the gum leaf serenade to Malcolm Turnbull and his entourage. Cruse is a significant member of the Eden community and performed a great rendition of 'We Are Australian'.

The caption from the *Daily Telegraph* website is: 'Malcolm Turnbull enjoys gum leaf serenade', but the pained expression on his face suggests everything aside from enjoyment.[5] And it's this moment that epitomises the campaign difficulties that Turnbull is experiencing: meeting the *hoi polloi* seems to be endured under sufferance, like the Tudor regal advised by his courtiers to meet with his subjects, to show the 'human side' of themselves but backfires because there was no human side to show. In the Eden experience, there's no enjoyment, it's more like a 'WTF' moment.[6]

Also appearing with Malcolm Turnbull is the sitting Member for Eden–Monaro, the Liberal's Peter Hendy, an apparatchik of the Australian Chamber of Commerce and Industry, previously Chief of Staff to former Howard government Minister, Peter Reith. He's a policy wonk, and is totally unsuited to be being a member of Parliament—he's invisible to the local community, and looks like someone that would prefer to be bunkered up in his campaign office, rather than be out on the streets talking to people. It's these types of sitting members of Parliament that are lead in the bag for Turnbull's campaign, and will continue to cause him grief over the next month.

*

5   Simon Benson, *Daily Telegraph*, 'Federal election 2016: Coalition to launch attack on Bill Shorten's $200 billion blowout', 23 May 2016. http://www.dailytelegraph.com.au/news/national/federal-election/federal-election-2016-coalition-to-launch-attack-on-bill-shortens-200-billion-blowout/news-story/c6a723bf12bacc3a38a4d0caf679be2a

6   SBS News, 'PM serenaded by Aboriginal elder during election campaign in NSW', 23 May 2016. http://www.sbs.com.au/news/article/2016/05/23/pm-serenaded-aboriginal-elder-during-election-campaign-nsw

Polls up to 28 May 2016

ReachTEL, 26 May 2016
LNP 48% | ALP 52%

Essential, 19–22 May 2016
LNP 49% | ALP 51%

Newspoll, 19–22 May 2016
LNP 49% | ALP 51%

ReachTEL, 19 May 2016
LNP 50% | ALP 50%

Ipsos, 17–19 May 2016
LNP 51% | ALP 49%

Morgan, 14–15 May 2016
LNP 47.5% | ALP 52.5%

Essential, 12–15 May 2016
LNP 49% | ALP 51%

Lonergan, 6–8 May 2016
LNP 50% | ALP 50%

Betting as at 28 May 2016

LNP $1.28
ALP $3.60

Prediction as at 28 May 2016

Labor Party to claim a two-seat victory.

Winning elections as easy as ABC

1 July 2016

In a perfect world, elections should be free and fair, and based on the relative merits of the policy proposals provided by each political party, presented in a balanced manner by the mainstream media, and then the right candidate wisely chosen by an attentive electorate.

Of course, this perfect world doesn't exist. The public generally has disdain for politicians and shows little interest in the electoral process, the media complains like attention-seeking toddlers about the election being 'boring' (*what, no nude dancing or fireworks?*), and information is severely distorted, where an unstable chaotic first-term government (two Prime Ministers, two Treasurers, two Speakers of the Parliament, 20 MPs resigning or retiring, and not one of its Budgets passed in Parliament) is reported as 'stable', and a Prime Minister with few economic credentials and making a hash of state–federal financial relations, is reported as having "the financial plan for the future". I realise that quoting George Orwell is a cliché in journalism, but this is classic newspeak.

Welcome to the real world, where well-established conservative interests dictate the way political information is presented to the public, and manipulate the media messaging to support their neo-liberal agendas. Hacks like Rupert Murdoch (who, after the *News Of The World* phone tapping scandals from 2006 onwards, should be spending time in jail) and Kerry Stokes (owner of The Seven Network) support spreading misinformation about centrist and left-of-centre, worker-based political parties, influencing public opinion through the media wherever possible. We're just lucky that mining magnate Gina Rinehart didn't have the skills or savvy to influence and control the Ten Network or Fairfax boards, otherwise, commercial media would be controlled by a maniacal trilogy of ego-centric entrepreneurs—two hacks controlling most of the media in Australia is bad enough, but having three would be insufferable.

However, as much as I dislike this, that's how the system works—ever since the days of American newspaper publisher William Randolph Hearst, money-people have lusted for the political power that comes with owning and controlling media interests. In Australia, at least there are some, albeit weak, legislative mechanisms that manage media concentration, although the Liberal–National Party is keen to reduce this legislation even further.

Previously, the ABC was somewhat in place to provide counterbalance and offer more nuanced reporting and critical analysis of the political news of the day—in the public interest. But, that's gone: ABC analysis has prominently leaned towards Liberal Party interests, ignoring many of their policy inadequacies and shortcomings, and magnifying any Labor issue or event that can be construed to be a negative—real or imagined, even if it just happens to be a flat tyre on the Labor Party's campaign bus (*geddit? Labor bus gets a flat tyre, just like its campaign that's running out of air! Hilarious!*)

Although I will provide some examples of this bias, I'm more intrigued about what has happened within the ABC for this to occur, an organisation which seems to have forgotten that it is a public broadcaster, and not a tool to be used to promote Liberal–National Party propaganda.

Last night's episode of *7.30* as an excellent sample. Its host,

Leigh Sales (who surely must be in line for a future Liberal Party candidacy or media position with the Liberals, like one of her former ABC colleagues, Mark Simpkin, who became Tony Abbott's Chief of Communications in December 2014), has been pushing Liberal's talking points that Labor's allegations of a Liberal Medicare privatisation plan is unfounded, and just a 'scare campaign', for an entire week.

Sales sniggered when Leader of the Opposition, Bill Shorten, said "I haven't given up winning this election and there's good reasons why I haven't given up winning it", and then proceeded to ask Shorten about leadership tensions and whether he'll face a challenge when he loses the election.[1] All on election eve!

In an earlier exchange during the campaign, ABC reporter Sabra Lane asked Liberal member of Parliament from the seat of Greenaway, Louise Markus, what her greatest achievements for her electorate have been. After an awkward 10-second silence, Markus explains that "all achievements are equally important", and then Lane helpfully provides a voiceover where she lists all Markus' porkbarreling projects.

In the absence of evidence, the ABC has developed a habit of broadcasting innuendo and unsourced claims (yes, usually against the Labor Party). On Friday night, ABC News 24 claimed Labor powerbroker, Senator Sam Dastyari, had withdrawn his support for Bill Shorten's leadership. Again, no names, no instances, just lazy speculation. For all we know, it could have been a story planted by Liberal sources. All put forward as serious journalism.

And, this theme of Shorten's leadership has been speculated by ABC News for three days, even though I'd suggest that it's Malcolm Turnbull who is under more leadership pressure, win or lose.

The Liberal Party promotions continued: On 1 July, reporter Anna Henderson, speaking about Malcolm Turnbull's

---

1   ABC Television, *7.30*, 'Interview: Bill Shorten'. http://www.abc.net.au/7.30/content/2016/s4492416.htm – see this exchange from 14:38 onwards.

appearance in the inner-west Sydney seat of Lowe: "The reception at a Liberal campaign rally was akin to a hero's welcome". This was a three-minute story, entirely positive to the Liberals, littered with victory references: Turnbull was there "to win over some last minute fans", and "the local candidate [Liberal Craig Laundy] was very confident of victory".

Funnily enough, there was no mention at all about Labor's candidate, Angelo Tsirekas. I did check, and he's definitely a candidate but, the ordinary and average viewer would have no idea. I've counted 12 stories on the electorate of Reid—not one has mentioned Tsirekas, and all stories have been highly favourable to Malcolm Turnbull and the Liberal Party. This is my local seat. Of course, I'll take more notice when it appears in the news, but ABC News reporting on many other seats has either neglected to inform the viewer about the Labor candidate, or reduced their impact by downplaying expectations.

Another segment on ABC News 24 provided a two-minute section of Turnbull spruiking all the benefits of a returned Coalition government, and the disaster of a Greens–Labor minority government. The segment concluded, with no outro or follow-up analysis by anyone. In the segment following, presented by reporter Andrew Greene, it lasted two-minutes and Bill Shorten spoke for around 30 seconds, with Greene adding his commentary: "a lot of questions still over what will happen to the Labor leadership if, as the polls predict, the Coalition wins.

"Overnight, we've also seen former Labor Prime Minister Bob Hawke weigh into the election at a private corporate event in Sydney ...it looks increasingly likely that the Coalition will win the election".

So, an opinion from an 86-year former Prime Minister at a private event—again, we never hear from the actual source, or what the context was—is more prominent than any other perspective. And, the polls are actually saying something different, and have been for some time, currently sitting at either 50:50, or 51:49 to Labor, based on current predictive preference flows.

This has been the narrative provided by ABC News for some time during the campaign: journalists Chris Ulhmann, Greg Jennett, Tom Iggulden, Sabra Lane, Leigh Sales, Fran Kelly, David Lipson, Michael Brissenden… (I could go on, but you get the picture) all have been singing from the same score sheet— *the polls are predicting a Coalition victory* (even though they are not), *Bill Shorten's leadership is under pressure, questions are being asked!* (even though his leadership is not under threat nor, aside from these fanatics, are questions being asked).

I've never before seen leadership speculation on a leader in the final week of a campaign—perhaps the journalists don't understand a political party is not going to change its leader in the week just before the election—but in the current environment at the ABC, any sort of gossip or hearsay develops a feedback loop in an echo chamber, and leads the news bulletins. If questions are being asked of Bill Shorten's leadership, why not of Malcolm Turnbull's? He leads a very divided party—where are the questions about how long he will last if he loses a swathe of seats, or loses the election?

Where are the questions about the Parakeelia scandal, where parliamentary expenses from Liberal members of Parliament were syphoned through this company back into Liberal Party coffers—$1.4 million since 2008/09, including $1.1 million over the past three years? Where are the tips and rumours of Senator Arthur Sinodinos' corruption and dealings with Sydney Water? Or the interrogation of Malcolm Turnbull's history at Goldman Sachs and his involvement with the downfall of HIH Insurance? Or the Panama Papers, where Turnbull's involvement in offshore investment schemes was too lightly brushed off?

As I queried before, why is there a collection of journalists— online, on radio, and on television—that are so keen to contrave the ABC Editorial Policies and Code of Practice[2], and install themselves as partisan hacks and political players?

During his time as Minister for Communications, Malcolm Turnbull, if he saw anything that enraged him, or anything that he saw was against the interests of the Liberal Party or the Coalition government, would pick up the phone and abuse the ABC Managing Director of the time, Mark Scott, pressure him to act, or suffer the consequences. This is classic rich tyrant man's bullying behaviour.

We saw this with the gagging of ABC Technology Reporter, Nick Ross, who wrote many analytical articles critical of the Coalition's NBN fibre-to-the-node and mixed-method-technology, especially in 'The vast differences between the NBN and the Coalition's alternative[3]' article, published in 2013.

At the time he was forced to move from the ABC, Nick Ross and his wife had just become new parents, but Ross was thrown onto the scrap heap for revealing the truth about the Coalition's vastly inferior and costly NBN plan. Turnbull was also behind the sacking of SBS journalist Scott McIntyre, for his tweets about Anzac Day in 2015.[4] Behind Turnbull's smiling façade is an inner tyrant. He wasn't known as 'The Ayatollah[5]' for nothing.

The neutering of the ABC commenced with the appointment of Jonathan Shier as Managing Director in 2001, and the stacking of the ABC Board by far-right supporters of the Liberal Party, such as Janet Albrechtsen and Maurice Newman, who have been

2   ABC, *ABC Editorial Policies: Principles and Standards*, http://about.abc.net.au/wp-content/uploads/2016/05/EditorialPOL2016.pdf

3   Nick Ross, ABC, *Technology and Games*, 'The vast differences between the NBN and the Coalition's alternative', 21 February 2013. http://www.abc.net.au/technology/articles/2013/02/21/3695094.htm

4   Lisa Visentin, *Sydney Morning Herald*, 'Sacked reporter Scott McIntyre and SBS resolve dispute over Anzac Day tweets', 11 April 2016. http://www.smh.com.au/business/media-and-marketing/sacked-reporter-scott-mcintyre-and-sbs-resolve-dispute-over--anzac-day-tweets-20160411-go37vt.html

5   Mike Steketee, ABC, *The Drum*, 'Is the Turnbull of old hiding below the surface?', 18 September 2015. http://www.abc.net.au/news/2015-09-18/steketee-is-the-turnbull-of-old-hiding-below-the-surface/6786056

very public in their disdain for the ABC. A 20-year campaign to change the culture of ABC political reporting has now reaped dividends for the Liberal–National Party. Journalists are fearful of losing either their jobs or their positions of influence so, they toe the party line of their paymasters. Either that, or the entire journalism team at the ABC has had the collective lobotomy and, suffering from Stockholm Syndrome, has relented under the stream of constant abuse and started loving their captors.

Whatever the reasons, the ABC reporting of the 2016 election has been shambolic, and biased to the extreme. Their journalists have given their own ABC code of conduct short shrift, and consistently lobbied on behalf of the Liberal–National Party. If the Labor Party happens to win the election, they should hold a night of the long knives, and clean out the partisan garbage from the ABC. In the public interest.

*

Polling up to 1 July 2016

Newspoll, 28 June–1 July 2016
LNP 50.5% | ALP 49.5%

ReachTEL, 30 June 2016
LNP 51% | ALP 49%

Essential, 27–30 Jun 2016
LNP 50.5% | ALP 49.5%

Galaxy, 28–29 June 2016
LNP 51% | ALP 49%

Ipsos, 26–29 June 2016
LNP 50% | ALP 50%

Essential, 23–26 June 2016
LNP 49% | ALP 51%

Newspoll, 23–26 June 2016
LNP 51% | ALP 49%

ReachTEL, 23 June 2016
LNP 51% | ALP 49%

Galaxy, 20–22 June 2016
LNP 50% | ALP 50%

Essential, 16–19 June 2016
LNP 49% | ALP 51%

Betting as at 1 July 2016

LNP $1.10
ALP $7.00

Prediction

Liberal–National Party – 77 seats
Labor Party – 67 seats
Australian Greens – 1 seats
Other independents – 5 seats

Of the last 46 published polls, the Liberal–National Coalition has led in 10 polls, Labor has led in 19 polls, and 17 have been even. Importantly, the Coalition has led three of the last five most recent polls.

The Coalition, as the media keeps telling us, has already won the election. The respective parties usually know on the Thursday night before the election how well they are likely to go. The last two state elections have gone against expectations (Queensland in 2015, Victoria in 2014). Federal elections tend to be more predictable, based on statistical volume that is available over a longer period time.

With the introduction of the Nick Xenophon Team, predictions could be wildly inaccurate. The Coalition will lose seats, but it's not sure if these will be claimed by Labor.

The Coalition should win, based on the numerical advantage they currently hold, but their campaign has been so woeful, and their term in office has been lacklustre, to say the least. Bill Shorten has easily won the three election debates, but who remembers those?

Labor has run a strong campaign, but there are too many conservative interests that lobby hard against them, including the ABC, who we can now safely say is conservative team player. Mission complete.

2016 election night and beyond

et's go back in time: it's the evening of 24 November 2007, and Labor leader Kevin Rudd is making his election victory speech at Brisbane's Suncorp Stadium. Aside from the speech being long winded and making odd references to Iced Vovos and cups of tea, it ushered in speculation of a long reign of Labor rule. And with good reason too. Soon, Labor would be in office federally, and in every state and territory, with the Lord Mayor of Brisbane, Campbell Newman, the most senior Liberal in the land. *Brisbane!*

Gradually, the bookshop shelves that had been peppered with tomes outlining how Labor lost its soul during its time in the wilderness, how could it survive as a party, and what type of future does it have, were replaced with books suggesting that it was the Liberal Party without a future, a declining membership base, a lack of interest, and questions about how could it possibly survive with its lacklustre new leader, Brendan Nelson.

In the post-World War II era, with the exception of the Whitlam governments between 1972–75, federal governments have held long-term tenures. The election of Menzies government in 1949 ended eight years of Labor rule; the Liberal–Country Party coalition was in office for 23 years; again for eight years between 1975–83; then Labor in office for 13 years, followed by the Howard government for 11 years. Four changes of government over a 60-year period. Governments with longevity have been the norm in Australia for some time, so the expectations that Labor would also follow suit under Kevin Rudd were quite reasonable.

At the 2007 election, the Liberal–National Coalition was thrashed. Labor secured a crushing election victory: a swing towards it of 5.44 per cent, 53.8 per cent share of the two-party preferred vote, a majority of 24 seats in the House of Representatives, as well as the sitting Prime Minister, John Howard, losing his seat, leaving the Coalition in disarray.

Listening back to Rudd's speech on election night in 2007, it's incredible to consider that within the space of nine years, we would see:

1. Three Liberal Leaders of the Opposition before the end of 2009—Brendan Nelson, replaced by Malcolm Turnbull who, in turn, was replaced by Tony Abbott.
2. Kevin Rudd, a first-term Prime Minister, removed by his own party, and replaced with Julia Gillard, three months before the 2010 election.
3. A hung Parliament at the 2010 election, the first result of this type since 1940.
4. Prime Minister Julia Gillard replaced by Kevin Rudd, also three months before an election, in 2013.
5. Tony Abbott becoming Prime Minister at the 2013 election.
6. Malcolm Turnbull challenging Abbott, and becoming Prime Minister in September 2015.
7. A double dissolution election in 2016, with the Liberal–National Party hanging on to office by one seat, and Pauline Hanson's return to Parliament, along with four new One Nation Senators.

After Australia had four Prime Ministers over a 32-year

period between 1975 and 2007, there was the unusual situation of five different Prime Ministers within five years, an instability that had not been seen in federal Parliament since the formative years of federation in the 1900s.

The real end of certainty

While he's not the sole architect of this political dysfunction, the point where Tony Abbott became Leader of the Opposition in December 2009 coincided with a run of seven years of unstable government. Firstly, Abbott ruthlessly exploited leadership division in the Labor Party and constantly depicted the proposed changes to the mining royalty system and carbon emissions trading systems as "Labor's big new tax". Standard politics, but Abbott took brutal 'whatever-it-takes' political strategies to a new level.

When Abbott led the Coalition to victory in September 2013, there was relief in the electorate that the Labor leadership games between Kevin Rudd and Julia Gillard were finally put to rest. The first words Abbott mentioned in his election victory speech were "Australia is open for business", but his new government proceeded to be anything but, slowly paced for the rest of 2013, dismantling as much of the Labor program as possible, and then proceeding to open up agendas that he never outlined to the electorate (such as the proposed $7 Medicare co-payment), or reneging on clear election commitments ("no cuts to health, no cuts to education, and no cuts to the ABC or SBS"), cocooning offshore immigration detention into bureaucratic secrecy and introducing 'on water matters' into the political vernacular.

There was not much substance to the Liberal–National Coalition's political agenda, surprising for a party that had spent six years in Opposition, and at least three years in a wilderness of soul-searching and attempts to define the relevance of the Liberal Party to a contemporary electorate.

Without a clear direction for which way the country was heading, Abbott reverted to an ideologue who was a hybrid

Prime Minister/Leader of the Opposition. The skills required to be Leader of Opposition are vastly different to the skills of Prime Minister and the requirements of government, but Abbott never made the transition to power as well as he could have, or as well as he should have.

One peculiar aspect of the 44th Parliament was that very early on in the term, the government had the feel of a long-term government that had run out of steam and run out of ideas. Aside from a grab-bag of right wing conservative ideals that not too many people are interested in and remain unpalatable to a large section of the electorate—such as repealing Section 18c of the *Racial Discrimination Act*—the government didn't really have much going for it. It was primarily a do-nothing government that never really left the levers of Opposition behind when it returned to office and, if it ever felt any political pressure coming on, it would usually reach for the 'stopping the boats' mantra.

During the first few months of 2014, it was difficult to distinguish the performance of the Liberal–National Party in government, and in Opposition—both modes were pugilistic; both modes were based on winning every single minor battle, but losing sight of the overall game plan; both modes were shrouded in secrecy and obfuscation; 'on water matters' and the behaviours of Minister for Immigration, Scott Morrison, the prime example of this.

With no clear agenda, Abbott chose to go down the nationalist and militaristic path. The two Australian flags that appeared at his earlier media conferences became four; which then became eight, and finally 10 flags by June 2015. Most political matters became either an emergency or a war on something, including a 'National Budget State of Emergency'; the creation of the Australian Border Force, with outfits and logos a seemingly odd combination of Darth Vader and a black-ops security firm; 'Operation Sovereign Borders', and the debacle of 'Operation Fortitude' on the streets of Melbourne.

Installed to government in 2013 with 90 seats and a majority of 30, obviously Tony Abbott had clear approval to govern, but not a mandate to introduce many of the severe measures introduced in the infamous Budget in May 2014. This Budget, also introducing the infamous 'lifters and leaners' by then Treasurer, Joe Hockey, was so severe and fiscally irresponsible, that it's no wonder it was blocked by the Senate (incidentally, it was never passed by the Senate, and neither were the 2015 and 2016 Budgets). Although the descent of Abbott had already commenced before this, Budget 2014 is the time his woes really started to set in and by mid-year, less than nine months after becoming Prime Minister, there were already whispers about when Abbott would be replaced, and who would replace him.

But, of course, when there is pliant conservative mainstream media willing to overlook any indiscretion, and unwilling to ask the hard questions, any fool of a Prime Minister can remain in office indefinitely.

However, for all of the meandering, misguidedness and ideological pursuits, none sharpened the barbs more that Abbott's decision to offer a knighthood to Prince Philip on Australia Day 2015. It showed that Abbott was not just yesterday's man, or from yesteryear, but from a sphere that no-one else had ever travelled to.

It was the day that marked the beginning of the end of Tony Abbott; unable to articulate who he really is or what his government stands for; engaged in petty pursuits of political opponents; and never going past the point of waging ideological battles from a bygone era. Abbott faced a leadership spill motion in February 2015 (which was defeated by 61 votes to 39); followed up with another failed Budget in May 2015; and finally ousted by Malcolm Turnbull in a leadership spill on 14 September 2015, where he lost the vote, 44–54.

Like the Greek myth of Icarus, Abbott had flown too close to the sun: not the golden sun, but the nefarious one and with his burnt wings, came crashing down, banished to the exile of the backbench, with a promise of 'no wrecking, no undermining, and no sniping'. It's odd that he felt the need to mention this, because no-one can ever believe that a Prime Minister losing a spill and the leadership would ever sit on the backbench and not feel the need to create the odd act of sabotage for his new leader, especially when Kevin Rudd had created the template for sniping when he lost the Labor Party's leadership in 2010.

Respecting people's intelligence

To say that there was relief when Tony Abbott was deposed as Prime Minister in 2015 is an understatement: *there was ecstatic jubilation*. Not in the same way that émigré communities celebrate when a much despised dictator in their homelands is deposed or dies, but an acknowledgement that we had just seen the end of a truly incompetent Prime Minister, who was now being unfavourably compared with the yardstick of incompetence, Bill McMahon, Prime Minister in the early 1970s. Abbott was in office for one day short of two years; at least he stayed in longer than McMahon, but not by much.

Once he became Prime Minister, Malcolm Turnbull didn't need to say much. He pulled the Liberal–National Party two-party preferred polling up to 57 per cent in late November (after being behind in 124 consecutive national polls from April 2014 to September 2015 and languishing at 43 per cent of the two-party preferred vote); and had massive personal approval ratings, reaching a preferred Prime Minister rating of 76 per cent in October 2015; and net approval ratings of +51 (Approval: 69 per cent, less Disapproval: 18 per cent).

A bedazzled media entourage lapped up every word: Malcolm was king, and it wasn't a question of whether he'd win the next election, but by how much, and how many decades he would be Prime Minister—retiring at the time of his own choosing, of course.

A Prime Minister anywhere near as good as the media made him out to be, would have announced an election in early October, and held it in late November 2015. I'd say that in that scenario, Turnbull would have probably held or increased the Coalition majority; Bill Shorten would have been replaced as Labor leader after this election and we'd again be talking about Labor facing another decade in Opposition. By prevaricating in the same way that Kevin Rudd did in early 2010 when faced with an option for a double dissolution election on climate change, Turnbull lost momentum, dithered and fell in love with the mellifluous tones of his own voice.

Narcissism trumped pragmatic politics and, as Turnbull would find out, there would be a large price to pay, in more ways than one.

If the end of 2015 represented a lost opportunity for Malcolm Turnbull, 2016 was shown to be a waste of time and a loss of political capital not seen in this country before. John Howard as Prime Minister, had the right strategy—his greatest virtue was that while he made many early mistakes, he learned from them and rarely made them again. But Turnbull never learned.

Turnbull's government meandered through the first few months of 2016, with various political flares thrown around to gauge public reaction: increasing the goods and services tax to 15 per cent; a bizarre plan to allow states to raise their own income taxes (even though this is not allowed in the Australian Constitution); speculation about when the election would be called—general or double dissolution? Would it be after or before the 2016 Budget?

Eventually, Turnbull agreed that 2 July 2016 was the best date for an election, and that both houses of Parliament would be dissolved. A media frenzy followed, with all the cool journalists bandying the 'DD' moniker, claiming yet more false dawns for Malcolm Turnbull, extolling the bravery and courage of a Prime Minister taking on a high wire risk, but assuring us all that his courage would be rewarded with electoral success.

Many in the media were predicting a small loss of seats, but a solid victory with an '8' in front of the amount of the seats won, meaning anywhere between 80 and 89 of the 150 seats in total. ABC journalist, Chris Uhlmann, confidently predicted on 15 June that "looking at the entire picture though, it still leaves Labor well short of government", and the Coalition was on track to win at least 80 seats. This was a theme picked up by all mainstream media, overlooking the consistency of all published polls that were pointing to a much closer election result. Professional journalism? Not at all, just evidence of unethical hacks and spivs pushing the agendas of their conservative masters.

Election day

So, what to make of election day 2016? The media was doing its best to concoct a leadership crisis for Bill Shorten; Fairfax Media journalist, James Massola, being the worst culprit, with more discredited rumblings published on 27 June, claiming that "some have begun to discuss Bill Shorten's future" and further claims the day before the election, that Sam Dastyari had withdrawn his support for Shorten, and thrown it behind Anthony Albanese. Why bother with 'fake news', when the supposedly reputable scribes at Fairfax Media are just plainly making the news up, and feeding gossip to their friends at other media establishments? Credibility? Zero.

So confident of victory was Malcolm Turnbull that he donated $1.75 million of this own money to the Liberal Party—on 1 July, so the news of the donation wouldn't be released by the Australian Electoral Commission until a year after the election—and stopped campaigning at midday on election day, and going for a leisurely public train trip to Parramatta, before returning to his Point Piper mansion to watch the election coverage on television.

As votes continued to be counted, Turnbull's confidence turned to gloom, and then to outright hostility. Seat after seat was lost by the Liberal–National Party during the evening, and it became clear that the result was going to be much closer than the mainstream media had anticipated (or hoped for), with many analysts on the night predicting a hung Parliament. When Turnbull eventually appeared at the Sofitel Wentworth Hotel in the Sydney CBD well after midnight, it wasn't a prime ministerial appearance of any kind. Turnbull was ropeable and the body language spoke a thousand barbed words: *How could you fuckers not choose me! I spent $1.75 million to get elected! Laaaabor… you wanted them instead of me!*

It was, without doubt, the most diabolical election night political speech from any state or national leader. It was embarrassing and demeaned the office of Prime Minister.

We started with Kevin Rudd's speech from 2007, a folksy tale that was as inspirational as watching varnish dry. But it was a kind-hearted, principled speech with some gravitas. Turnbull in comparison, was akin to the spoiled bully boy without his expected prize at a school academic speech night, overturning chairs, abusing people and giving the middle finger to everyone, including his supporters.

He lashed out the "an extraordinary act of dishonesty," claiming that Labor had tricked people with text messages to voters in marginal seats with "Mediscare" messaging. "No doubt the police will investigate," he said. Afterwards, the Liberal Party lodged a complaint with the Australian Federal Police but, in August 2016, the AFP stated that the matter was "evaluated by the AFP [and] no Commonwealth offences were identified. This matter is now considered finalised and no further comment will be made." Turnbull's response was: "if that wasn't a crime, it should be one."

Back to election night at the Sofitel Wentworth: No thanks were offered by Turnbull to the Australian electorate for exercising their democratic right to vote, or the usual platitude about how Australia is the model of excellence for having free and fair elections and, unlike some countries, no blood spilled onto the streets. There were no 'thank yous' to the Liberal Party stalwarts all around the country that set up the polling booths the night before, hoping to persuade voters to their cause. No thanks to all of the candidates that risked their careers to run for the Liberal and National parties. No commiserations to the Liberal and National Party members of Parliament that had lost their seats—14 of them. Although they never gain public sympathy, these are emotionally difficult times for losing members of Parliament, yet not a word of public thanks from their leader on election night.

And then Turnbull turned his attention to the putative reason for the double dissolution election—the Australian Building and Construction Commission legislation—a matter that was barely raised during the election campaign.

Looking at all the evidence, Turnbull's strategy and campaign for 2016 was a disastrous failure and showed a deep lack of judgement. The end result was a loss of 14 seats (90 seats, down to 76), a swing against the Liberal–National Party of 3.13 per cent, a loss of three Senators—resulting in more independent cross-benchers to deal with in the Senate, making key legislation even more difficult to pass.

The media become so engaged with Turnbull's musings that they forgot to consider what the public thought, and so thoroughly dismissed polling showing the election was going to be close, that they were stunned into silence when the Liberal–National Party was returned to office with a slender one-seat majority.

The mainstream media failed miserably in overlooking the incompetence of Tony Abbott, and were even more irresponsible in failing to point out the many failings of Malcolm Turnbull.

Politics is eating itself

Whenever politics is seen as being in the doldrums, waiting for the next Nietzscherian Superman (*Übermensch*) to arrive on the stage and redeem the future, there are clarion calls for a re-invention of the political system; it's broken, it needs to be fixed. But the system itself is not broken—after all, the constitution has functioned perfectly well since 1901 (except for the 1975 constitutional crisis and the sacking of Prime Minister Gough Whitlam), and the method for managing Parliament and electing its representatives is a good system.

But, it's the character of the people that move to politics, and the party institutions that make up the Parliament. Public trust in the political system is low, according to many polls,[1] and many electors say members of Parliament are greedy, personally corrupt, put themselves and their political parties first, and see personal aggrandisement as their primary purpose in politics.

How difficult is it for members of Parliament to update their pecuniary interests register after purchasing an investment million property, as former Minister for Health, Sussan Ley, managed to avoid in early 2017? Ley continued to spin the fib that she purchased a $780,000 luxury apartment on the Gold Coast as a 'spur of the moment' decision, while on parliamentary business. Evidence came out that she had made several enquiries about the property beforehand, and the real estate agent that she made the purchase through is a prominent figure within the Liberal Party, as well as substantial donor to the party. Several months later, Minister for Employment Michaelia Cash also failed to declare a $1.4 million property purchase, saying that she was "mortified" about the oversight.

Mortified? How stupid do they think the electorate is?

Parliament should be reflective of the community, and there'll always be charlatans unable to resist the temptation of rorting their travel allowances, or stretching the boundaries of the rules of entitlements. But parliamentarians are also meant to be role models for acceptable behaviour in society, not reflections of old-styled aristocracy, where public monies are splurged at whim.

Many people have asked me about the causes of this instability over the past decade, but it's difficult to pin-point it

---

1   Margot O'Neill, ABC *Lateline*, 'Poll data reveals Australia's waning interest in politics, decline in support for democracy', 12 August 2014. http://www.abc.net.au/news/2014-08-11/poll-data-reveals-waning-interest-in-politics/5662568

to one key factor. For Labor, the key personalities were in the backroom—former National Secretary Karl Bitar, and former politician Mark Arbib—not real Labor people, but factionalised people interested in ratings, polls, group research, personalities, self-aggrandisement and trouble making. Where is Mark Arbib now? After four years as a Labor Senator (2008–12), he's now a senior executive with James Packer's private investment company, Consolidated Press Holdings. And Karl Bitar? After the disastrous 2010 election campaign and resigning as National Secretary in 2011, Bitar became the chief government lobbyist for Crown Limited—yes, also owned by James Packer—and is now Executive Vice President of Crown Resorts. They were Labor, but they may have well been working for a tuna can factory. They ruined the Labor Party for a generation and now work for one the biggest benefactors and supporters of the Liberal Party.

Former Labor member of Parliament Martin Ferguson is another. Supported by the union movement and the Labor Party for most of his life, Ferguson was a senior figure in the Rudd government, holding several key industry portfolios. He left Parliament at the 2013 election, and took up lucrative lobbying positions within the mining and tourism sectors, taking pot-shots at Labor policies and criticising any Labor leader on climate change and mining issues that were detrimental to the industries that he now represents.

Although not in the federal sphere, former NSW Premier, Mike Baird, resigned from office in January 2017. Although he clearly stated that he was retiring from politics due to 'family reasons' and to spend more time with his children (which are all perfectly valid reasons), the following month, he took up a senior position with the National Australia Bank, on a salary of $1 million, with the potential to increase to $2 million. So much for wanting to spend more time with the family.

As at July 2017, Labor is well placed to form government at the next federal election, due before November 2019. But Labor provides hope to the electorate, in relative terms, mainly because the current Liberal–National Party is so inept at government, and is headed by a Prime Minister that has disappointed the electorate so much, that even with a very supportive mainstream media, it is difficult to see how long he will survive for.

Will the cynical cycle of politics continue if Labor is returned to office after the next election? The template for dissent and destructive politics was created by Tony Abbott in 2009 when he became Leader of the Opposition, and his reward was becoming the Prime Minister and returning the Liberal–National Party to government in 2013. The double-edge sword is that not only was he ill-equipped for the role of government, but he also created a vacuum for his own demise. Any future Leader of the Opposition will closely look at this time and be tempted to implement such a destructive path, even if the reward is the prime ministership and a return to government for just a couple of short years, which, surely, is far better than languishing in the misery of Opposition, away from the limelight. Meanwhile, the political wellbeing of the nation can take a back seat.

Australia, along with many other countries in the world, faces great economics challenges, along with the future of food and energy resources, employment, education, and technological change. The main question facing Australia's political system is whether the current personal within Parliament are the right ones to face these great challenges.

*

Eddy Jokovich is an independent journalist, political analyst, media producer and award-winning publisher, based in Sydney. He analyses politics one vote at a time.

@EddyJokovich

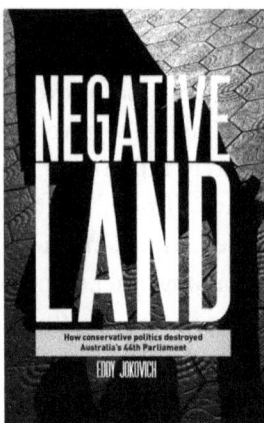

To order more copies of this great book:
newpolitics.com.au/nl-order

To purchase the e-book for Kindle:
newpolitics.com.au/nl-kindle

Like or don't like the book? To post a review on Amazon:
newpolitics.com.au/nl-amazon

www.ingramcontent.com/pod-product-compliance
Lightning Source LLC
Chambersburg PA
CBHW050730030426
42336CB00012B/1495